Outcomes, Performance, Structure (OPS)

Three Keys to Organizational Excellence

Outcomes, Performance, Structure (OPS)

Three Keys to Organizational Excellence

Michael E. Gallery, Ph.D., CAE, FASAE
and Stephen C. Carey, Ph.D., CAE, FASAE

ASQ Quality Press
Milwaukee, Wisconsin

American Society for Quality, Quality Press, Milwaukee, WI 53203
© 2014 by ASQ
All rights reserved. Published 2013.
Printed in the United States of America.

18   17   16   15   14   5   4   3   2

Library of Congress Cataloging-in-Publication Data

Gallery, Michael E.
Outcomes, performance, structure (OPS) : three keys to organizational
excellence / Michael E. Gallery and Stephen C. Carey.
    pages cm
ISBN 978-0-87389-870-6 (hardcover: alk. paper)
1. Organizational effectiveness. 2. Performance. 3. Total quality management.
I. Title.
HD62.15.G354 2014
658.4'013—dc23
                                    2013041418

Acquisitions Editor: Matt T. Meinholz
Managing Editor: Paul Daniel O'Mara
Production Administrator: Randall Benson

ASQ Mission: The American Society for Quality advances individual,
organizational, and community excellence worldwide through learning, quality
improvement, and knowledge exchange.

Attention Bookstores, Wholesalers, Schools, and Corporations: ASQ Quality
Press books, video, audio, and software are available at quantity discounts with
bulk purchases for business, educational, or instructional use. For information,
please contact ASQ Quality Press at 800-248-1946, or write to ASQ Quality Press,
P.O. Box 3005, Milwaukee, WI 53201-3005.

To place orders or to request ASQ membership information, call 800-248-1946.
Visit our Web site at www.asq.org/quality-press.

∞ Printed on acid-free paper

Quality Press
600 N. Plankinton Ave.
Milwaukee, WI 53203-2914
E-mail: authors@asq.org
ASQ   The Global Voice of Quality™

To Michelle Mason, CAE, FASAE…our good friend and colleague whose vision, support, and encouragement made this book possible.

Contents

List of Figures and Tables

Foreword

The fact that you have chosen to read this book tells me that you and I share a few things in common. We are both interested in ensuring that the organizations with which we are involved are as effective and as efficient as possible. Which begs the question: How do we know?

As is true of nearly all my colleagues in association management, I entered this field from a different one. I was trained in the science of human performance improvement. As with other academic disciplines, there was a body of knowledge to which I could turn to find answers and there were questions to which there were no current answers. Equally important, I was provided with a system for identifying problems and, in a disciplined way, discovering answers, from someone else's research, their educated opinions, or my own research and opinions.

As an association executive for 23 years and a consultant for the past seven, I have found very little discipline in the way in which management in general, and association management in particular, has developed their respective bodies of knowledge. Writing for the *Journal of Association Leadership* in 2006, I stated: "...Management literature has often fallen into the trap of awarding unmerited currency to new ideas simply because they are new. Ideas should survive because they advance new understanding of how to better manage associations. To achieve that we {must} use all the tools available to us, particularly the underused tool of science."[1]

As I followed the literature in association management (and organizational management) while also attempting to keep current with my field of human performance improvement, I continued to be troubled by the lack of rigorous inquiry and debate in the field of management. One fad simply seemed to be followed by another. More troubling to me was the fact that large association meetings invited speakers from the for-profit world to come and share their experience with us. To be sure, these meetings had a forum for association executives to present; however, the keynote addresses always came from outside the field.

Disheartened but not defeated, I continued to explore the literature. I was one of the millions of readers who were fascinated with Jim Collins's book, *Built to Last,* published in the early 1990s. Finally, a book resulting from a disciplined research approach! I was equally thrilled to read his subsequent book, *Good to Great.* Curious person that I am (Collins refers to such persons—himself included—as chimps; it certainly sounds better than chumps), I wondered to what degree his findings would apply to the non-profit world. For example, Collins found that the CEOs of great for-profit companies get the right people on the bus...and the *wrong* people *off* the bus. CEOs of non-profits have two buses, a leadership bus and staff bus. They have a great deal of control over the latter and little, if any, with the former. I wished and hoped that our field would conduct a project in the association management world similar to what Collins had done. As luck would have it, early in 2003 I was chair of the research committee for the ASAE Foundation. A very good friend and extremely bright chimp, Hugh Lee, FASAE of Fusion Productions, was hosting a meeting featuring Jim Collins. Hugh was also very interested in seeing a similar "good to great" study done with non-profits, so he invited me and others to sit down and talk with Jim at the meeting. That meeting became the catalyst for one of the greatest adventures of my life.

Jim was eager to assist us in the project but made it clear from the outset that he did not wish to do any of the work. He would gladly serve as our mentor but the heavy lifting would be up to us. Michelle Mason, as staff member with the ASAE Foundation at the time, got things rolling. Ginger Nichols, chair of the foundation, appointed me chair of the project and gave me *carte blanche* to select the rest of the committee. In addition to Hugh and Michelle, I was lucky to get some of the finest minds in the profession to become a part of the team. Their names appear prominently in the front of *7 Measures of Success: What Remarkable Associations Do That Others Don't,* the book that was a result of the project.

After rigorously studying nine great and nine good associations over three years, we found seven things that great associations do and good ones don't do. As evidence of the association executives' desire for research-based answers, to date, more than 30,000 copies of the book have been sold.

In reviewing *7 Measures,* it became very clear that it also complemented the process used in the Malcolm Baldrige Award for Performance Excellence, to stimulate thought in how best practice organizations are managed. The program is based on time-honored management principles and recognizes outstanding organizations that adhere to those criteria. In 2005-06, the program was extended to include organizations in the non-profit sector. A variety of nonprofits from hospitals, government organizations, and other institutions have been recognized.

Although the literature began to provide answers on what great *looked like,* there were no guides on *how to become* great. It was then I had my "ahah!" moment. What had I been practicing for more than 30 years? Human performance improvement! Organizations are composed of humans. Organizational performance is the combination of human performance. The answers could be found by applying those principles and practices to association management.

This book is not an "answer book" in the sense that we present a series of common problems and the accompanying answers. To be sure, many such books exist—such as *101 Ideas for (fill in the blank).* Most of these answers are based on someone's recollection of what they did to solve a problem. The results of the solution, measureable gains, are seldom if ever reported.

This book provides a system for discovering your own problems, developing solutions, evaluating success, and gathering information that will help to improve solutions should they fail on the first attempt. It is based upon more than 30 years of research within the discipline of human performance improvement.

On behalf of my co-author and dear friend Stephen C. Carey, who contributed the "thought" questions in each chapter based on Baldrige principles, and myself, I want to extend a very sincere "thank you" for placing enough trust in us to read this book. We hope that once you are finished reading it, you come to the conclusion that we earned that trust.

Michael Gallery
Highland Village, Texas 2013

1

Keys to Excellence

INTRODUCTION

Any organization is faced with answering some fundamental questions: Why do we exist? Whose needs will we meet? Which needs? How will we meet them? How will we measure success? Some organizations go about answering these questions in an orderly, systematic way; many answer these questions in a haphazard way. The former group of organizations is far more successful than the latter.

There is no shortage of written material describing the characteristics of highly successful organizations. Jim Collins and Jerry Porras provided one of the first data-based books offering a glimpse into what great for-profit companies shared in common and distinct from merely good companies when they published *Built to Last* in the early 1990s.[2] A few years later, Collins published *Good to Great,* where he again used a data-based approach to describe the common characteristics of good for-profit companies that became great as compared to their counterpart companies that simply remained good.[3]

Additionally, in 2005 Collins re-emphasized these points in "Good to Great and the Social Sectors," his monograph to accompany *Good to Great.*[4] He argued that good-to-great principles apply to the social sector as well, as indicated by data gathered in his research with more than 100 social sector leaders.

Also in 2005, The American Society of Association Executives (ASAE) and The Center for Association Leadership published *7 Measures of Success.*[5] The book reported on a three-year research study lead by a team of association executives who studied nine remarkable associations and compared them to nine good ones. The team discovered seven characteristics that remarkable associations shared and that the nine good associations did not possess.

Since 1987, the criteria for the Malcolm Baldrige National Quality Award (since 2010 referred to as the Baldrige Performance Excellence Program) have been widely available.[6] The Baldrige Criteria for

Performance Excellence offers organizations an integrated approach to managing with a focus on delivery of ever-improving value to customers and stakeholders, contributing to organizational sustainability, improved organizational effectiveness and capabilities, and organizational and personal learning. The Criteria, in fact, form a Performance Excellence Framework that connects and integrates each of the key management elements an organization needs to reflect and act upon to be successful.*

All of these works provide key questions and excellent benchmarks against which organizations can measure their own performance. The problem is not with assessing where an organization might be falling short, but with knowing how to effectively solve those problems once they are illuminated. None of the books mentioned above were designed as "how to" sources. They do not offer, nor were they designed to offer, suggestions for how an organization might develop the characteristics of highly successful organizations described in their texts.

Certainly, there is no shortage of "how to" books. Scores of authors offer numerous books filled with suggestions on how to better run an organization. Many executives buy those books and implement the ideas offered. Often, those ideas fail to bring about the change promised in any long-term way. That is not to say that none of those ideas work. Many of them do. The difficulty lies in implementing change in a systematic way, verses a piecemeal way, to bring about long-term, effective change.

Many of us have had the experience of going to a store and purchasing a barbeque grill. When we get it home, we discover that what we have really purchased is a box of parts. It doesn't become a functioning barbeque grill until the parts are properly assembled. So it is with our organizations. Many of us have a "box of parts"—a mission statement, some goals and objectives, a business plan with carefully developed strategies. Unless, however, we carefully assemble these parts so they work together toward the same end, our organizations will not function properly. Any attempts to fix problems in isolation, rather than in the context of the entire organization, are also likely to fail.

We view organizations as systems. A system, simply defined, is the interaction of parts that, working together, produce an outcome that no single part, working independently, could produce on its own. Let's consider a simple example—an association's annual meeting. The education committee can develop high quality program content. However, all the quality will be lost if the meeting management team does not ensure that the program is implemented in a quality meeting

---

* The authors draw on the Malcolm Baldrige Criteria for Performance Excellence to supplement and lend force to key issues brought up in the text, and to pose key questions in each of the chapters that readers can use to thoughtfully review what they currently do in their own organizations. The questions are formulated from the Malcolm Baldrige Criteria for Performance Excellence. For further information on the Baldrige program, please visit their website at: http://www.nist.gov/baldrige/

site. And none of that will happen if the promotion and marketing team does not properly communicate the value of the program to potential registrants. Whether these functions are done by several people in a large association or by a small group of people in a small association, all these parts must come together to produce a quality program. No one part, acting independently, can produce the same outcome that all the parts can produce collectively.

Seems obvious, doesn't it? Yet when problems arise, those problems are almost always the result of the parts not working together. Fixing a problem in isolation will not resolve the problem. Consider registering people for a conference. One of us used to manage a large professional association. The annual meeting for that association averaged more than 5,000 registrants. One year, an outside housing company was used to assist registrants with booking their hotel rooms for the meeting. Registrants completed their registration on the association's website and called a number provided by the website to help with the hotel booking. The booking agent had only one concern—booking a room. When there were no longer any rooms available, the agent informed the registrant. This usually resulted in the registrant canceling his/her registration. Clearly, we had a major customer service issue. A problem in one area—hotel registration—was affecting other parts of the system and also negatively affecting one of the association's objectives: increasing registration. Developing an effective solution required looking at all parts of the system. Procedures were put in place so that if the room block became 90% full, the housing company alerted the association meetings department so that additional hotel space could be obtained. Further, the name of any registrant with a concern about housing was taken by the housing company and provided to the association so that an association staff member could follow-up with the person. The registrant was *our* customer, not the housing authority's.

OPS: OUTCOMES, PERFORMANCE, AND STRUCTURE

The idea of looking at organizations as systems has been around for more than 40 years. Karl Ludwig von Bertalanffy got things started with his book, *General Systems Theory.*[7] His work led to the development of a new interdisciplinary field referred to as Human Performance Improvement (HPI). HPI is composed of trainers, psychologists, engineers, and economists, among others, who are interested in bringing about organizational change. While elaborate models and themes can be developed, they all boil down to three essential elements that we refer to as OPS: **O**utcomes, **P**erformance, and **S**tructure. The Human Performance literature leads us to conclude that although each element is important, for purposes of planning and problem solving, it's best to "think backward"—first to the outcomes we want, then to performance we need to attain those outcomes, and finally to structure. Let's take a closer look at each element.

Outcomes

The word *outcomes* refers to why the organization exists and what it produces. An organization's mission statement (and, for some organizations, also their vision statement) as well as its goals and objectives are statements of outcomes. Moreover, they are all gradually more specific. For example, a state dental association's mission is to "help (State) dentists succeed." This statement encompasses a rather broad range of potential activities. The association also has identified six objectives over the next three years in pursuit of that mission:

1. Increase reserves by 20%
2. Increase non-dues revenue by 10%
3. Obtain 80% market share of new dentists and 70% of dental students
4. Obtain 78% market share of all dentists
5. Increase the number of members involved in the association and increase the number of qualified leaders
6. Achieve 90% member satisfaction

These objectives provide a more specific statement of desired outcome, within the framework of the organization's overall mission of helping dentists succeed. When a new idea is proposed, the board can determine whether that idea falls not only within the mission, but within the organization's objectives as well. Poorly constructed mission statements and ill-defined objectives make this job much more difficult. For example, it is not uncommon to for an association to develop a goal of having the association be the center of information for its members. There is nothing wrong with having such a goal; however, there is everything wrong with stopping at that level. The goal as written is rather unclear. How, for example, will the association leadership determine if the goal has been achieved? In the absence of a more specific statement of intended outcome, the expectations of one group within the organization may be different from the expectations of other groups. Such a situation will only lead to friction—not success.

Focusing on outcomes first helps the board effectively address some of the key organizational questions we mentioned at the outset. Why does the state dental association exist? To help dentists in that state succeed. Whose needs will we meet? Dentists in that state.

Performance

An organization engages in certain activities to produce identified outcomes. A statement of strategies, activities, and programs refers to performance. In other words, it refers to what people, both staff and volunteers, do on a daily basis to produce outcomes. Those organizations with loosely defined outcomes become activity driven. Activities become an end in themselves. Such organizations have difficulty cutting programs; in the absence of a clear direction, any idea will do. In these organizations, many times the activity with the strongest voice behind it will win the day. Without clear and common understanding of the organization's purpose and the outcomes it seeks to achieve, evaluating one product, activity, or service against another becomes a very difficult job. So, job #1 of the performance function is to assist the association in identifying at what level each of its objectives needs to be sustained in order to create the desired outcomes.

Structure

After defining desired outcomes and identifying the strategies (performance) to achieve those outcomes, leaders must evaluate whether structures are in place to facilitate performance. When outcome and performance are not clearly defined, no one structure is any better or worse than another. No single right structure exists for all organizations. As the old saw goes, "form follows function." Consider a large for-profit wine distributor that uses a model in which two sales people are assigned to a set of stores to sell wine. The two sales people are told they are partners and instructed to work together as a team. Each person has a separate list of list of wine to sell. Each is paid commission based on the wine sold from their individual list. The managers of the company consistently lament that their sales force is not working as a team. No kidding! The company has created a structure that rewards *individual* performance, not *team* performance. The structure does not support the desired performance.

Let's look at another example. It is not uncommon for professional associations to have both a board and a house of delegates. Often the house of delegates, which meets once or twice a year, has final authority over both policy and budget. How many business owners would create a structure in which major business decisions were made by a group of individuals who met once or twice per year? In this case structure does not support the process of efficient and effective decision making.

SUMMARY

What will this book do? We will *not* develop new criteria; those are in place with Baldrige criteria and the *7 Measures*. The purpose of this book is to help you put those criteria in a context of your organizational system and assist you in using the criteria to assess problems in your organization. Human performance improvement specialists define *problem* as a critical (that is, important) difference between "what is" and "what should be." More importantly, this book will help you in designing systemic solutions to the systemic problems you have identified with easy-to-use samples and questions that draw out key areas where the organization needs to improve. We have found that most organizations are not lacking in information. What is most often lacking is a framework that leaders can use to organize and make sense of the information they have. We will provide a framework through OPS. We will also help you engage in "backwards thinking" as you attempt to identify—and fix—real-world problems with practical solutions.

2

Outcomes and Backwards Thinking

OPS MODEL

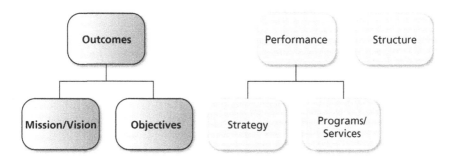

PRE-ASSESSMENT

Prior to beginning this chapter, answer each of the questions below, marking the corresponding box for yes, no, or don't know (DK). If you answer "yes" to all of the questions, we suggest you might want to quickly review this chapter and move to the final section entitled "OUTCOME EVALUATION." If you answer "no" to any of the questions, the material in this chapter will be helpful to your organization in correcting the situation.

Question	YES	NO	DK
Does the organization have a clear statement of what it does and why it exists?	☐	☐	☐
Does the organization have clearly stated, specific, and measurable outcome statements?	☐	☐	☐
Does each outcome statement represent a reasonable stretch from what the organization has achieved in the past?	☐	☐	☐
Are the organization's outcome statements consistent with its mission and goals?	☐	☐	☐
Does the organization conduct a formal evaluation annually to assess whether its outcomes have been achieved?	☐	☐	☐
Does the organization use evaluation data to modify outcomes and activities?	☐	☐	☐
Does the organization have no more than six to eight major objectives at any one time?	☐	☐	☐

CHAPTER OVERVIEW

In this chapter, we will be discussing how to evaluate organizational outcomes. Said simply, we will assist you in determining whether your organization is producing what it intends to produce. Remember: a problem is a critical difference between what *should be* and *what is.* Identifying problems concerning outcomes requires that your organization has specified its intended outcomes in specific, measureable terms—a statement of what should be. Secondly, your organization has gathered objective data on its actual outcomes—what is. Comparing the actual data with the organization's stated desired outcomes help you identify "outcomes" problems, if any exist. This chapter focuses on helping you identify problems in the outcomes area.

A SYSTEMS APPROACH TO ORGANIZATIONAL PROBLEM SOLVING

The systems approach to problem solving is both systemic and systematic.[8] Problems are not identified or addressed in isolation. Instead, problems are viewed within the context of OPS, Outcomes, Performance, and Structure. As we discussed in the first chapter, your organization might not be generating the number of new members it wants (an outcome problem). The reason for that problem may be related to a lack of an effective and comprehensive membership campaign (performance); the lack of the right message to the right audience (performance); the lack of sufficient volunteers to recruit new members (structure); or all of the above.

This problem-solving approach is also systematic in that it follows the principle that Jim Collins discovered about great organizations. Namely, that they are made up of disciplined people, doing disciplined things, in a disciplined way. The approach we present in this and succeeding chapters will help you systematically go about the business of finding what problems exist and what actions you need to take (and in what order) to correct them. Let's be clear from the outset: we are not offering magical solutions. We frankly don't know of any. What we are offering is a data-driven process that will enable you to develop your own solutions to your own problems and measure your own success. If the corrective measures you put in place fail, the process we offer will help you analyze the failure and improve the solution. No magic…just a lot of hard work.

BACKWARDS THINKING

The three elements of the OPS approach to problem solving are outcomes, performance, and structure. Most often this is pictorially represented as shown in Figure 2.1.

Figure 2.1   Three elements of the OPS approach to problem solving.

When you are planning and problem solving with the OPS approach, it is important to think backwards, starting with the end in mind (outcomes).[9] Once your organization is clear about what you are trying to achieve, you can then plan what people in the organization will do (performance) to achieve those outcomes. Finally, your organization can use the planned process to develop structures that must be in place (budget, people, policies, and so on) to support the planned work. The planning and evaluation process would look like that shown in Figure 2.2.

Figure 2.2   Backwards planning with the OPS approach.

OUTCOME PLANNING: DESCRIBING WHAT SHOULD BE

Mission Statement

The most basic element of outcome planning is a clear statement of why the organization exists—a mission statement. The literature makes it very clear that one of the hallmarks of great organizations is that they are mission driven. They have a clear sense of mission and they do not engage in activities outside of that mission.

Successful organizations create a series of filters through which ideas flow. The first and most broad filter is the organization's mission, a concise statement of why the organization exists. The second filter is the organization's statement of goals and objectives, a more specific outline of what the organization seeks to accomplish in carrying out its mission. When a new idea or opportunity arises, successful organizations first ask: Does pursuing this idea fit our mission? If not, they reject the idea. If it does fit the mission they ask: How will this idea help us accomplish our goals and objectives? In the absence of this process, those ideas championed by the strongest voice often win. The organization will travel in a zigzag course, moving from one strong voice to another. Successful organizations hold their course on a straight line toward their stated mission and objectives.

Successful organizations also have a clear idea of their customer. A customer is defined as a person or entity that pays a fee in exchange for a product or a service. Retailers understand that their customer is the end user. Wholesalers understand that their customer is not the end user but the retailer. Associations and non-profits often confuse the customer with the beneficiary. Many physician associations, for example, put the patient at the center of their mission statement. However, patients do not buy their products and services. Physicians do. The physician is a customer of the physician association. The patient is a beneficiary. Some would say that sounds self-serving. We would argue that members pay dues to an organization to be served. To deny that is to fail to understand who the customer is and why they pay dues.

Not only is it important to know who the customer is, it is also critical to know your organization's value proposition. What are you offering that customers want to buy? A value proposition can be defined in terms of meeting a customer's unmet want or solving a customer's unresolved problem. Notice we use the term *want*, not *need*. Often leaders recognize that the customers they are trying to serve need something long before the customers themselves realize the need. However, unless a "want" is created, customers will not buy it, regardless of how much they might need it. And "need" should not be confused with "like." Many of us want insurance, but we don't like buying it.

So, in summary, successful organizations begin with defining why they exist…in the context of the customers they serve and the value proposition they offer.

Paul Niven tells us, "the mission isn't just window dressing: in fact, the very success of public and nonprofit enterprises is often dependent, at least in part, on the development of a crystallizing mission."[10]

If a mission statement is going to meet that purpose, it needs to be concise, easy to understand, and easy to communicate. Most of all, it needs to serve as the driver for organizational behavior. Some organizations try to write a mission statement to please all stakeholders. What they often end up with is a long mission statement that really says very little—or one that says so much that any activity can be justified.

Think of a product or service that you highly value. Do you know that company's mission statement? Do you care? The primary audience for the mission statement is the board and the staff; they are the ones who will use it. Whenever a new idea comes forward, the first question all within the organization evaluating the idea should ask is this: Is that idea consistent with our mission?

Consider the following examples of clearly stated mission statements:

- American Psychiatric Foundation: Overcoming mental illness, advancing mental health, and eliminating stigma

- Florida Medical Association: Helping Florida physicians practice medicine

- International Order of the Golden Rule: Making independent funeral homes exceptional
- Solar Energy Industries Association: Build a strong solar industry to power America

All these examples are concise and easy to communicate. More importantly, they serve as a first filter for an organization.

Exercise 2.1

We suggest that before writing a mission statement, your organization address the following questions:

1. Who are our customers and who are our beneficiaries?

2. What key unmet wants or unsolved needs do our customers face?

3. How do we increase the quality of life for our customers and beneficiaries?

4. How do we provide an appropriate return on the financial and human resources we expend?

Using the answers to the questions above, write a succinct statement (one or two sentences) that clearly identifies the value proposition your organization offers to its customers.

Mission Statement:

_____

_____

_____

Goals and Objectives

When engaged in planning, people often are confused as to the difference between goals and objectives. *Goals* are defined as aspirational statements of desired ends. They are not necessarily meant to be achieved. Rather, they are something the organization continually strives to attain. While many organizations have goals, some make the mistake of stopping at that level. Consider the example we used in the last chapter: "Our organization seeks to be *the* center of information for our members." This is a laudable goal. It states an aspiration that will probably never be achieved, but one that is constantly reached for. The goal serves little purpose, however, if the organization does not further define what it specifically hopes to achieve. If it is left simply as a goal, how will the board and staff determine whether the organization is, in fact, *the* center of information for its members? Does the organization only consider itself successful if virtually all members have this view of the organization, or will most suffice? If so, what constitutes most? And how is "information" defined? All information? Key information? Without further definition, organizational leaders are left to their own devices in answering these questions, and each may arrive at a different answer. So, it's fine to include organizational goals as long as the organization develops specific objectives that further define their intended outcome for each goal.

Balanced Score Card (BSC) Approach

When attempting to define organizational objectives, many organizations struggle with determining what areas they should address and how many objectives they should have. Robert Kaplan devised the balanced score card approach several years ago.[11] Although it contains many of the principles of systems thinking, many find the process very cumbersome and time-consuming. That said, we do find the underlying approach helpful for planning outcomes. The notion behind the BSC approach is to focus on three key areas: finance, the customer (member), and the organization. In order to effectively meet our mission, what must we accomplish financially? What customer needs must we meet? And, what organizational changes do we need to make to be more effective?

We think of the BSC approach as three legs of a stool. If the three legs are not in balance, those sitting on the stool will rock...and perhaps even fall. An organization can make decisions that, in the short term, help the bottom line but hurt the organization and its customers in the long term. Consider airline companies that charge for bags; good for the bottom line, but not so good for the customer. Or consider the company that, in the face of declining profits, "right-sizes" and cuts staff. In the short term, expenses are reduced, but so is capacity. Eventually the organization is less able to meet customer needs. Some organizations discount member dues. That's good for the member, but not so good for the organization's bottom line. More often than not, discounts do not result in increased members; they decrease revenue and eventually reduce member service. Some organizations attempt to offer products and services that members want, but the organization has no capacity (or competency) to deliver.

Keeping these three elements in balance helps the organization provide customers what they want, what the organization can afford, and what it has the capacity to deliver. Our approach will assist you in defining goals and objectives in these three areas.

Being SMART

For more than 30 years, thousands of organizations have benefited from using SMART objectives.[12] The acronym stands for: specific, measurable, achievable, relevant, and timely Let's discuss each element separately.

Specific involves identifying what you are going to accomplish. Let's assume that assessment data indicate your organization needs to focus on increasing revenue. As we have already discussed, the simple statement "increase net revenue" is a goal statement. Will any increase at all mean success? Think in terms of our own personal lives. Most of us would like to become more physically fit. That said, we haven't said much. For such a goal to have meaning—to guide our behavior—we must be more specific. We should commit to something specific: "lose 20 pounds in the next 4 months" or "reduce my blood pressure to at least 125/80 in the next 30 months." Specific statements leave no doubt as to what you intend to accomplish. In the case of net revenue, we might have a statement such as "increase net revenue 3%/yr. for the next three years" or "increase non-dues revenue by a total of 8% in three years."

Measurable means just what it says. The organization commits to objectively determining whether it has accomplished its desired outcome. It has been aptly noted that the absence of measurement results in the absence of management. If there is no measurement, there is no accountability. If there is no accountability, there is no management. Therefore, once you have identified specifically what you wish to achieve, you will then want to identify how you will know if you have succeeded. What measures will indicate success?

Some things are easy to measure directly. Let's consider our personal fitness example above. We can measure directly whether we have successfully lost 20 pounds or lowered our blood pressure. Other things are not so easy to measure. Consider, for example, "responsibility." All of us want staff members who are responsible. But we can't measure responsibility as directly as we can weight. In these cases, we use what measurement experts refer to as "indicators."[13]

What behaviors would indicate that a person is responsible? Examples include showing up to work on time, completing assignments by the deadline, and accepting criticism. We use these indicators as measures of the presence or absence of responsibility.

An association that seeks to increase organizational adaptability poses a similar challenge to that posed by measuring responsibility. Although we can directly measure whether programs and services have been dropped, it is more of a challenge to determine whether the right programs and services have been dropped. Let's stay with our example of organizational adaptability. How might the organization measure whether it has dropped programs that fail to meet member needs?

It might decide to use the following indicators to determine that all programs meet the following criteria:

- We have data to document the need addressed by the program.
- At least 10% of the members use the program or service.
- At least 80% of those using the program or service agree the program or service addresses their needs.

Achievable refers to the organization's reach. You will want to set realistic, achievable targets. When setting targets, it is important to recognize the difference between safe bets, stretch goals, and pipe dreams. Safe bets represent a continuation of the present. If you have had an 80% retention rate in membership, a target for 80% next year is a safe bet. A stretch calls for extending your current resources to achieve a higher (but potentially reachable) standard. In this case, you might set a target for achieving an 83% retention rate next year. A pipe dream speaks for itself—something nice to wish for but extremely unlikely to happen. Moving from an 80% retention rate to a 95% retention rate next year would be a pipe dream for most organizations.

Once your organization has set targets, consider carefully the organization's current performance. Does the movement from the present position to the target represent a stretch? Is it a safe bet or a pipe dream? You may wish to modify your target to ensure it is achievable.

Relevant means the target is related to a documented need and that it fills a verified gap between what is and what should be. You want to ensure that the objectives you select are going to address critical organizational issues.

Timely ensures that the time for addressing the outcome is now rather than later. In other words, of the myriad of things your organization could be doing, are these the things you should focus on now?

In addition to having SMART objectives, the organization must have a reasonable number of objectives. The literature makes clear that high-performing organizations are focused on doing a few things well. It is extremely difficult to focus on and manage more than six to eight organizational objectives. One of our clients complained that the board had assigned her twenty-three priority objectives. Twenty-three priorities is an oxymoron!

Exercise 2.2

We have discussed the three legs of an organizational stool: finance, membership, and organizational capacity. We would suggest the following goals for each area.

- Finance: Strengthen and diversify the financial foundation of the organization

- Customers (membership): Provide greater value to customers (members)

- Organizational capacity: Increase organizational effectiveness

Goals: Write a goal statement for each of these areas, using our suggestions or replacing it with a statement that better fits your organization's needs.

Finance goal:

_____

_____

Customer (membership) goal:

_____

_____

Organizational capacity goal:

_____

_____

SMART Objectives: As we have discussed, goal statements identify an aspiration. It is important for the organization to identify in specific, measureable terms what it intends to accomplish relative to each of the goals it has set. Most organizations have moved to a three-year window for planning. For each goal, write no more than two specific, measureable, achievable, relevant, and timely objectives for your organization to accomplish within the next three years.

1.0 Finance

1.1 Objective

_____

_____

1.2 Objective

_____

_____

Exercise 2.2 *(continued)*

2.0 Customer (Membership)

2.1 Objective

_____

2.2 Objective

_____

_____

3.0 Organizational Capacity

3.1 Objective

_____

_____

OUTCOME EVALUATION

The purpose of outcome evaluation is to assess the degree to which the organization is meeting its desired outcomes. The evaluation should address the following questions:

1. Does the organization have a clear and concise mission statement that puts forth the organization's value proposition to its customer(s)? If not, develop a mission statement that does.

2. Does the organization have no more than six to eight SMART objectives, specifying in measureable terms what it intends to accomplish over a three-year period in carrying out its mission and advancing towards its goals? If not, develop SMART objectives that do.

3. Do the organization's SMART objectives address the need to balance between finance, customer (member), and organizational capacity? If not, develop SMART objectives that achieve such a balance.

4. Assuming questions 1-3 are in the affirmative and further assuming that the time period for the objectives has ended (i.e., three years have elapsed), ask the following question for *each* objective: Is there clear and convincing evidence that the measure stated in the objective has been met? If yes, then the organization can replace that objective with a new SMART objective. If the objective has not been met, then further analysis is required. Guidance for that analysis begins with the next chapter.

3

Defining Performance: Strategies for Success

OPS MODEL

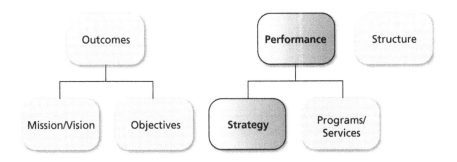

PRE-ASSESSMENT

Prior to beginning this chapter, answer each of the questions below, marking the corresponding box for yes, no, or don't know (DK). If you answer "yes" to all of the questions, we suggest you might want to quickly review this chapter and move to Chapter 4. If you answer "no" to any of the questions, the material in this chapter will be helpful to your organization in correcting the situation.

Question	YES	NO	DK
Are the major programs and activities of the association consistent with both the organization's mission and its objectives?	☐	☐	☐
Do the organization's leaders demonstrate an ability to redirect resources, as needed, based upon an evaluation of the environment?	☐	☐	☐
Are market research data used as a basis for developing and revising programs and services?	☐	☐	☐
Do organization leaders demonstrate openness to alternative options for achieving the desired end?	☐	☐	☐
Do organizational leaders demonstrate a clear understanding of the market segment it serves?	☐	☐	☐
Does each part of the organization recognize the role it plays as well as the roles of other parts of the organization in achieving organizational objectives?	☐	☐	☐
Are cross-functional teams used to develop and implement organizational strategies?	☐	☐	☐
Are failed strategies analyzed and revised accordingly?	☐	☐	☐

CHAPTER OVERVIEW

The organization has clearly defined why it exists (mission statement) and what it plans to achieve over the next three years. The organization has also documented its current status. This chapter will focus on ensuring the organization is doing the right things...in the right way. We will first discuss developing broad strategies that will serve as the organizational glue that binds organizational activity. In subsequent chapters, we will discuss techniques for developing specific tactical plans that are consistent with the organization's objectives and core strategies. Further, we will provide a framework for organizations to evaluate current programs and services and we will offer methods for evaluating the success of strategies and tactics.

SOME DEFINITIONS OF TERMS

Terms such as "strategy" and "tactics" are common to most of us. What is less common is a shared definition of those terms. For our purposes, strategies define what will be done and tactics define how the strategy will be accomplished.[14] Let's consider an example. Currently 50% of Association XYZ's revenue comes from non-dues. Over the next three years, the organization seeks to increase that percentage to 60%. Before getting bogged down in the details of specific programs and services that it might offer to reach this objective, the organization must first step back and determine a general approach—a strategy it will use to guide it in the development and implementation of specific products. The association has several options, including:

1. Increasing the net revenue of current products and services by increasing prices

2. Identifying and developing new markets for current products and services

3. Decreasing the costs associated with producing and marketing current services

4. Developing new products and services for existing markets

Generally, strategies involve cutting (option 3) or building (options 1, 2, and 4).[15] An association may elect to use some or all of the strategies above. Let's assume, in our example, that the association selects strategy 4. It would next identify specific products to develop and implement. Those products would be considered tactics for implementing strategy 4.

DEVELOPMENT OF STRATEGIES

Frankly, the data on the successful implementation of strategies are not very encouraging. It has been estimated that 60% to 70% of strategies fail to achieve their intended outcome.[16] We suggest that is not an argument for not developing strategies; rather, it is an argument for developing and implementing strategies in a disciplined way. Some of the reasons strategies fail include:

1. *Inadequate understanding of the strategy:* The more complicated the strategy, the less likely it is to be implemented. Strategy statements should be simple and communicated clearly.

2. *Lack of buy-in:* Successful strategies must have the support of the board as well as of those who will implement them. Within an association, that means staff and volunteers. When staff and volunteers are involved in the development of strategies, they are more likely to not only understand them but to implement them successfully as well.

3. *Lack of time:* As we have cautioned, it is important not to try to do too much at one time. Organizations that focus on implementing a few key strategies at a time will be more successful than those that try to be all things to all people.

Organizations can increase their chances of success in implementing strategies if they focus on the following:

1. *Alignment:* Ensuring that strategies align with the mission, objectives, and documented needs of the organization. Organizations are more successful when they avoid overreaching their capabilities. An association cannot successfully solve every issue that members face. Moreover, other organizations may be better suited than your association to solve certain issues. Focus on those strategies for which you do have the resources (both financial and human).

2. *Capacity:* Members have many needs and wants, usually far more than an association can effectively meet. Successful organizations focus on doing a few things well. They also focus on those things they have the capacity to deliver. In other words, they focus on those things they have the budget, the organizational talent, and the competency to create.

3. *Timing:* It is critical that the organization not be too far ahead of its members. Members may need a particular program or set of services, but do they want it? Of all the things that the association could be focusing on, are these the right strategies on which to focus right now? Are they the most crucial?

PROPER STRATEGY SELECTION

Strategies should emanate from the organization's mission and objectives as well as from an assessment of the organization's strengths, weakness, opportunities, and threats (SWOT). The organization should also look at other macro-environmental factors such as demographics, key issues, economics, and more. Much has been written about SWOT analysis and the exercise is familiar to most organizations.[17] Rather than discussing how to complete a SWOT and environmental analysis, we will focus on how to use the results to arrive at successful strategies.

Properly selected strategies enable an organization to focus on its strengths, neutralize is weaknesses, and capitalize on opportunities that become available. By engaging in a disciplined process of strategy evaluation, an organization can focus on those strategies that set it apart from its competition.[18] Companies in the for-profit sector have always faced stiff competition. Increasingly, associations find themselves competing with other associations as well as for-profit companies to provide products and services to members. As our society has become more specialized, associations serving a general category of membership have faced increasing competition from organizations that address the specific needs of a subset of the general association's membership. Historically, associations have offered members a sense of community as well as a central source of information. Social media and the easy access to information on the Internet serve as alternative sources for what has been the traditional value proposition for many associations. Therefore, the careful selection of well-though-out strategies becomes increasingly critical to an organization's success. Finding your "strategic niche" is a "must do" in today's competitive environment.

Strategies should help an organization focus on its competitive advantage, that aspect of the organization that sets it apart from its competition. Lexus sells cars, a product offered by a variety of competitors. Quality in engineering, service, and luxury set it apart from other car manufacturers in its price range. McDonald's sells hamburgers, as do hundreds of other companies. Fast, consistent delivery of an inexpensive product sets it apart. Many department stores offer product lines similar to those sold in Nordstrom, but few offer Nordstrom's level of service.

What does your environmental analysis reveal about your strengths, that is, your competitive advantage? Some of the possibilities you might consider are:[19]

- Speed of access
- Information "packaged" to meet the needs of a defined sector of membership
- Customer (member) focus
- Price advantage
- High quality
- Mass customization/simplification
- Value added (e.g., assembling available information and repacking it in a usable format for members)

Exercise 3.1

Working with key staff and volunteers, identify your association's key competitive advantage(s). You need not have more than one and you should not have more than three. If, during your discussion, you identify more than three, work with the group to identify the top three.

We noted earlier that strategies are either reductive or additive. Organizations should not only capitalize on their strengths but also mitigate, as much as possible, their weaknesses. In addition to selecting a strategy that capitalizes on your strengths and sets you apart from your competition, you will want to select strategies that help you deal with identified weakness including cost reduction, removal of redundant services, simplification of governance and management processes, reduction of waste, and elimination of energy drainers.

We suggest identifying no more than three core strategies on which to focus. Trying to implement more than three will only lead to frustration and failure. The selection should emanate from an environmental assessment that includes the participation of key staff and leaders. A core strategy builds on your competitive advantage and minimizes your organization's weaknesses. Core strategies cut across functional units (e.g., education, advocacy, certification, membership, and so on) and provide a focus for each of these functions. They are the "glue" that binds organizational activities together. Examples of core strategies include:

1. Making data-driven decisions about programs and services.

2. Enhancing our value proposition and being member/customer focused in all that we do.

3. Streamlining our product/service development process.

4. Leveraging and focusing on our strengths.[20]

Exercise 3.2

Selection of core strategies: Work with leaders and staff to develop no more than three core strategies. In doing so, work with the group to address the following questions:

1. What is it that we do well? What are we known for? (Or what do we wish to be known for?)

2. What can we do better than our competitors?

3. In what areas do we struggle? Where do we have consistent problems?

4. Where do we receive complaints?

5. What environmental factors will help us achieve our mission?

6. What environmental factors will hinder our ability to achieve our mission and objectives?

Once you have selected no more than three core strategies, the next step will be to identify critical actions to be taken in the coming year toward achieving those strategies. A long-range plan is just that: long range. All of the organization's issues will not be resolved in the first year. Therefore, it is critical for the leadership to identify what it will accomplish in the first year to advance the organization in the desired direction.

In addition to developing two to three core strategies, you will also want to develop functional unit strategies. Associations with large infrastructures will often be divided into major divisions and departments; smaller organizations may have staff who wear several hats. Regardless of size, most associations are typically divided into a variety of functional areas including education, communications, membership, and advocacy. Often, association committees composed of volunteers are also engaged in activities and projects related to these functional areas. We suggest that strategies be developed for each of these key areas, in line with the organization's mission and objectives, integrating volunteers and staff as appropriate.

As with core strategies, less is better. The more strategies developed, the more complex the management task and the less likelihood of success. Focus on doing a few things well. Volunteer leaders (e.g., committee chairs) and staff should work cooperatively to develop one to three key strategies for each functional area.

In an earlier example, we discussed that Association XYZ had an objective to increase non-dues revenue to 60% of its total revenue in the next three years. Several functional areas may contribute to this objective including education and communication. Each functional unit is asked to develop strategies for increasing net revenue. We have developed a format for strategy developed that many organizations have found useful (see Figure 3.1). As you can see from the form, the assigned group is asked to briefly describe the proposed strategy, indicate why they believe the strategy will help achieve the objective, describe the major steps involved in implementing the strategy, identify resources that will be needed beyond money and people's time, and finally to provide a ball-park estimate of the cost of the strategy (including staff time). This last element is not a meant to be a detailed budget but rather a best guess as to the total cost. Knowing whether a strategy is a $5,000 project or a $50,000 project will help leaders make better decisions later on.

Performance Specification Sheet Instructions

Your task force has been assigned the responsibility for developing a plan to accomplish the following organizational objective: [objective]

Please use Figure 3.1 to document the plan. We would like your task force to tell us:

1. What will be done to complete the objective? This is a brief statement of what will be accomplished (e.g., develop an educational program, develop a brochure, develop and distribute talking points, and so on). If there are multiple products, services, or activities, please list them all.

2. Provide a brief explanation of why you believe the suggested activities will help the organization successfully accomplish the objective. We recognize there are several ways to accomplish a task. Why did you select the suggested option? If you have any marketing or membership data to support your proposed course of action, please refer to it in this section.

3. Please list the specific major steps you will engage in to accomplish the proposed course of action. For each step, tell us who will be responsible for completion of the step and estimate the amount of time, in weeks, each step will take.

4. Indicate any special resources the project would require. For example, if you were proposing a book, the project would need an author with expertise in a particular subject matter. When in doubt, include rather than exclude potential resources.

5. Provide a ballpark estimate of the cost (excluding staff time and overhead) you estimate it would require to complete the proposed project. If there are multiple projects, please provide an estimate for each project. Providing a range (e.g., $30,000 to $35,000) is acceptable. Remember, however, that too a large a range limits the usefulness of the estimate.

6. Please submit your completed plan by (date).

Performance Specification Sheet

Objective:

_____

_____

Date:

_____

Completed by:

_____

Brief statement of strategy/tactics (what will be done to achieve the objective?)

_____

_____

Brief rationale (why do you think this will work?)

_____

_____

What steps will you engage in and how long will each step take?

_____

_____

Steps: Person responsible: # of weeks:

_____

What special resources, other than volunteer and staff time, will you need?

_____

_____

Estimated cost:

_____

Suggested metrics:

_____

Figure 3.1   Performance Specification Sheet.

STRATEGY SELECTION

Once all the strategies have been developed, the senior management team (in larger associations) or the executive director and the executive committee (in smaller associations) must next decide which strategies to select. Leaders (both staff and volunteers) must make their decisions based on: a) which strategies they believe best address the organization's mission and objectives, b) which strategies the organization can afford, and c) which strategies it has the capacity to deliver. We suggest leaders use the following set of questions to guide their thinking.

Strategy Evaluation Questions

1. Does the organization have individuals with the knowledge and skill required to carry out the strategy? If not, can it obtain the services of people outside the organization who do possess the requisite knowledge and skill?

2. Has the organization been successful in similar ventures? Has it ever successfully implemented similar strategies?

3. Does the organization have the resources (e.g., budget, technology, policies and procedures, and so on) in place to support the strategy? If not, does it have the potential to acquire those resources?

4. Can the strategy be implemented in a reasonable timeframe?

5. Does the organization have the will to see the strategy through?

6. Is the strategy critical to the success of the outcome?

Selected strategies provide the basis for identifying and selecting tactics. Tactics refer to the specific things an organization will do to achieve the objective. The *who, what, when, where,* and *why* should be spelled out, along with a budget. That will be discussed in the next chapter.

BALDRIGE CRITERIA
SUGGESTIONS AND QUESTIONS

The Baldrige Criteria for Performance Excellence asks you to consider the following questions when evaluating strategy selection. How do your strategic objectives:

- Address your strategic challenges and advantages?
- Address your opportunities for innovation in products, in operations, and in your business model?
- Capitalize on your current core competencies and need to identify future competencies based on your current and future environment?
- Balance short-term and longer-term opportunities?
- Consider and balance the needs of all stakeholders?
- Enhance your ability to adapt to sudden shifts in your market conditions?

Given great leadership, the answers to these questions about strategy development will set up your ability to focus on your customer and workforce, and assist in creating an operational focus to provide measurable results.

4

Evaluating Strategies

PRE-ASSESSMENT

Prior to beginning this chapter, answer each of the questions below, marking the corresponding box for yes, no, or don't know (DK). If you answer "yes" to all of the questions, we suggest you might want to quickly review this chapter and move to the final section entitled "SUMMARY." If you answer "no" to any of the questions, the material in this chapter will be helpful to your organization in correcting the situation.

Question	YES	NO	DK
Has the organization determined whether it has the capacity to implement a proposed strategy?	☐	☐	☐
Has the organization carefully analyzed what a proposed strategy will cost, both in terms of finances and human resources?	☐	☐	☐
Do organizational leaders and staff demonstrate a clear understanding of the markets they serve?	☐	☐	☐
Are market research data used as a basis for developing and revising programs and services?	☐	☐	☐
Do organization leaders demonstrate openness to alternative options for achieving the desired end?	☐	☐	☐
Does data on members' wants and needs, as well as what they value, serve as a basis for the organization's decisions on strategies?	☐	☐	☐

(continued)

Question	YES	NO	DK
Does each part of the organization recognize the role it plays, as well as the roles of other parts of the organization, in achieving organizational objectives?	☐	☐	☐
Are staff throughout the organization involved in major planning activities?	☐	☐	☐
When failure occurs, does it undergo proper analysis and improvement?	☐	☐	☐
Is experimentation encouraged?	☐	☐	☐

CHAPTER OVERVIEW

The organization has clearly defined why it exists (mission statement) and what it plans to achieve over the next three years. The organization has also documented its current status. Moreover, the organization has identified core strategies as well as functional area strategies to achieve its desired outcomes. The purpose of this chapter is to provide more detail to those strategies. We will assist you in answering such questions as these: What will be done...by whom, and when? What are the costs associated with implementing each strategy?

CREATING AN OPERATIONAL PLAN

Operational planning is rightly the responsibility of the staff rather than the board of an organization. The staff is in the best position to determine what resources are required, how those resources will be obtained, and what they will cost. Sometimes, in smaller or micro associations, operating committees act as or work in conjunction with staff for operational planning. For most associations, this section will guide the staff through that process.

STAFF ANALYSIS

Once proposed strategies have been developed, the staff should develop an action plan for each by addressing the following questions:

1. What steps must be taken to implement the strategy and in what order? List the major steps of the strategy. If one step is a prerequisite to another step, be sure to list the steps in proper sequence.

2. Who will be responsible for each step? Identify the individual who will be accountable for accomplishing the step. If more than one person is working on a step, list one person who will be accountable for the group. Remember, lack of accountability leads to lack of action.

3. When will the steps be accomplished? We have found a Gantt chart to be a useful tool for depicting project steps and their timelines.[21] A Gantt chart is provided in Figure 4.1. To complete the chart, list the steps in the far left column. Use a bar to show the timeline for continuing activities with the left end of the bar starting on the start date and the right end of the bar extending to the completion date. Use an X to mark the date of an activity occurring at a specific point in time. More information on Gantt charts and other useful project management tools can be easily found on the internet.

4. How much time will be required of each individual involved? Assessing whether the organization has sufficient human resources (both volunteers and staff) is a major challenge for both board and staff. When planning a major strategy, it is critical to identify how much time will be required to complete it. This information assists the board and staff in determining how many strategies it can effectively handle in a given period of time.

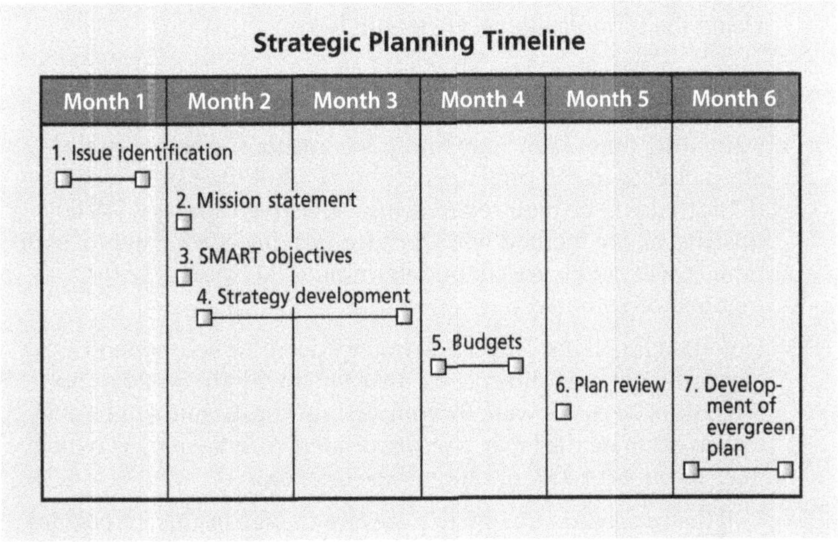

Strategic Planning Timeline

Month 1	Month 2	Month 3	Month 4	Month 5	Month 6
1. Issue identification ☐——☐					
	2. Mission statement ☐				
	3. SMART objectives ☐				
	4. Strategy development ☐———————☐				
			5. Budgets ☐———☐		
				6. Plan review ☐	7. Development of evergreen plan ☐——☐

Figure 4.1 Gantt chart example.

Staff should estimate the number of work hours required of each person involved. If no one in the organization has worked on a similar project in the past, arriving at an estimate of time will be more difficult than for activities that are common for the organization. Nonetheless, it is important to try to provide an estimate so you can determine whether people will have the necessary time to complete assigned tasks. A time-tested and effective formula for estimating time comes for the Performance Evaluation and Review Technique (PERT) developed years ago by the US Navy.[22] That formula is:

Time Estimate = $(O + (4 \times ML) + P)/6$

Where:

O is most optimistic estimate of time

ML is the most likely estimate of time

P is the most pessimistic estimate of time

Let's look at an example. Suppose you are trying to estimate the number of hours it will take a staff member to complete a project report. If all went very well, you believe the staff person could complete the report in one day, or 8 hours. Usually, all does not go well. The staff member will probably have to call members to follow-up on information and secure additional data. Therefore, you estimate that most likely it will take 12 hours to complete the report. If nothing goes right, it might take as much as 20 hours. Using the formula above, we would have:

$(8 + (4 \times 12) + 20)/6 = 12.66$

Although the work hour is the most accurate unit of measure for estimating time, some may find it too arduous. Another useful alternative is to compute the percent of a full-time equivalent (FTE) that will be required to complete a given strategy. While this alternative method will work for arriving at estimates of staff time, it will not be useful for determining the amount of time required of volunteers.

5. How much will the proposed strategy cost? We recommend capturing not only direct costs associated with the strategy, but the indirect costs as well. By completing Step 4, staff will be able to also estimate the labor costs associated with the project, which may account for 45% or more of the total cost.

6. Will the proposed strategy require any change in current policies and procedures? When discussing new strategies and plans, it is not uncommon for someone to say: "We can't do that; our policy

won't allow that." Or maybe, "Our procedure is not to do things that way." Policy should facilitate function, not the other way around. Some of the strategies may, in fact, not be aligned with current policy or procedure. The purpose of the review at this stage is not to raise a red flag to block those strategies, but rather to highlight a misalignment. When facing such misalignment, the board and staff can weigh the cost–benefit of changing policy or procedure to accommodate new ideas with the option of not moving ahead and staying with current policy and procedure.

Consider the following example. XYZ Association has a goal to have its procedures be more customer-driven. Members have clamored for an installment system for paying dues. Current policy requires that members pay their dues in full within 60 days of receiving the invoice. The board must now decide which alternative better serves the organization, keeping with the current policy or changing the policy to allow for installments.

7. Does the strategy call for technology the organization does not currently have? Perhaps the board has proposed a strategy that is beyond the organization's current capabilities. Let's stay with our example of providing members the opportunity to pay their dues in installments. Leaving policy issues aside, the organization may not have the financial software to enable it to provide this option. Software could be obtained, but the cost of acquiring that capability must be factored into the board's decision as to whether to move ahead with the strategy.

8. Will staff and/or volunteers need to learn new skills to implement the strategy? One of the questions we suggest organizational leaders address when reviewing strategy options is: Has the organization ever done anything like this before? If not, implementing the strategy may require staff and volunteers to learn new skills. The cost (and the time associated with that training) should be factored into the analysis of the project.

9. Will you need outside resources? Many associations, particularly those with small staff, must rely on outside resources to accomplish certain strategies (e.g., developing marketing materials, developing and implementing a survey). The time needed to acquire those resources as well as the cost of obtaining those resources should also be factored into the analysis.

At this point, the board has the facts before them, as best as those facts can be known. The board must now decide how feasible each strategy is. Decisions will be driven by the organization's culture. How tolerant is the organization of risk? Has it ever tried something like this before?

How much is known? Can the board build in some go/no-go decisions? Does the proposed strategy fit the organization's mission? Is the risk of doing something greater than the risk of doing nothing? It is important to remember that you will be able to assess and revise as the strategy is undertaken.

We strongly urge the board to remember that less is more. The organization will not move from its present position to remarkable overnight. Organizations tend to try to do too much too soon. Consider, for example, a person's desire to "get fit." As we all know from personal experience, trying to eat less, exercise more, and quit smoking—all at the same time—is usually a formula for failure. We do much better trying to tackle one issue at a time. The same holds true for organizations.

Jim Collins explains this best with his discussion of the flywheel. He notes that change comes about slowly at first. Disciplined people, doing disciplined things in a disciplined way. They push the flywheel and with great effort it begins to move slowly. With consistent effort, it will gradually but surely gather speed. Eventually, it will gain momentum and move faster with less effort. Trying to spin too many flywheels at the same time only results in exhaustion—and failure.

SUMMARY

The purpose of this section is to determine whether the organization is trying to shove ten pounds of "stuff" into a five-pound can. Perhaps stated more accurately, the organization is trying to determine how much "stuff" it has and how big a can it needs. To accomplish this task, we suggest the following:

1. The analysis needed for this step should be conducted by staff rather than volunteers.

2. Staff should develop a work plan.

3. Determine who will complete the strategy; be specific.

4. Use a Gantt chart or a similar method to depict what will be done and the timeline for those steps.

5. The board should evaluate the proposed work plans, using the discussion questions we have provided, and select a few plans that offer the greatest potential for success.

BALDRIGE CRITERIA
SUGGESTIONS AND QUESTIONS

In the planning phase, the Baldrige Criteria for Performance Excellence ask you to consider a number of questions when creating your operational plan. How does your operational focus address the following areas:

- What are your short-term and longer-term action plans and how are they tied to your strategic objectives?

- What planned changes must take place internally and among your strategic partners based on the plan design?

- How do you ensure the proper resources are identified and availability determined?

- How do you ensure the key outcomes of your plan are sustained?

- How do you manage financial and other risks that are associated with and identified in the plan?

- How will you establish and implement modified action plans if circumstances require a shift in plans or execution?

These fundamental and logical questions when viewed with the information above will ensure your plans are realistic and address all the key components necessary for a successful execution.

5

Managing the Organization's Portfolio of Activities

OPS MODEL

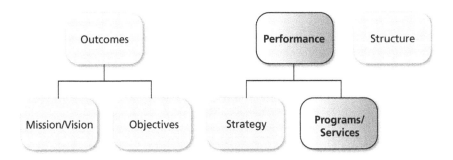

PRE-ASSESSMENT

Prior to beginning this chapter, answer each of the questions below, marking the corresponding box for yes, no, or don't know (DK). If you answer "yes" to all of the questions, we suggest you might want to quickly review this chapter and move to Chapter 6. If you answer "no" to any of the questions, the material in this chapter will be helpful to your organization in correcting the situation.

Question	YES	NO	DK
Are the major programs and activities of the association consistent with the organization's mission, vision, and objectives?	☐	☐	☐
Are programs evaluated to determine whether they successfully meet member needs?	☐	☐	☐
Are market research data used as a basis for developing and revising programs and services?	☐	☐	☐
Do you drop or revise programs that are not meeting member needs?	☐	☐	☐
Do organizational leaders demonstrate a clear understanding of the market segment the organization serves?	☐	☐	☐
Does the organization routinely collect data that tell them what customers need and want?	☐	☐	☐
Are customer service levels tracked routinely by measuring customer satisfaction with our products, services, interactions, and so on?	☐	☐	☐
Are failed strategies analyzed and revised accordingly?	☐	☐	☐
Does the organization have some products and services that generate revenue but are not related to our mission?	☐	☐	☐
Are marketing strategy and planning considered key to product delivery?	☐	☐	☐

CHAPTER OVERVIEW

We have noted that great organizations are marked by disciplined people doing disciplined things in a disciplined way. Part of that discipline calls for people to move systematically from a statement of mission and objectives to a specification of strategy and tactics. At this point in the process, we have a mission and vision statement, objectives, and a set of strategies, all core to establishing our operational framework. Also, we have developed our operational plan for implementing those strategies. Now it is time to focus on specific activities (i.e., tactics) the organization will employ to carry out its strategies and achieve its objectives. It is not uncommon for associations with which we have worked to begin strategic planning by discussing activities. For many, in fact, strategic planning is a process of listing and prioritizing organizational activities. By now, it should be apparent that without a clear statement of mission and objectives, it is impossible for an organization to have a meaningful discussion of priorities. In the absence of a clear and common understanding of where the organization is headed, it is difficult to know which activities should stay and which should go. When mission and objectives do not guide an organization, external pressure rather than an internal compass ends up driving it.

Activities are critically important. They define the organization and it is through activities that organizations are known to members and others. We are judged not by what we say but by what we do. Therefore, an organization's activities must be consistent with its vision and mission.

DEVELOPING AN ORGANIZATIONAL ACTIVITY PORTFOLIO

Some organizations do not know what they know. In other words, it is not uncommon for some members and staff to be so focused on their narrow realm of activity that they become unaware of the total scope of activity of the organization. Also, any activity, when viewed in isolation, may be viewed as successful. However, activities do not occur in insolation. Working on an annual meeting takes resources away from working on something else. Therefore it is important to first identify the total scope of activities and list them so each can be viewed in terms of its respective value to the organization as a whole.

In developing this important list, this question often arises: What is an activity? We believe the list should capture every project, product, program, or service the organization provides. Specific meetings and publications are obvious activities. But what about activities that are less easy to "count," such as advocacy and public relations, for example? Advocacy, like meetings and publications, is a broad label for common activities. We suggest listing major projects or initiatives within advocacy that account for significant amounts of time. Also, there are certain activities, such as supervision and budget development, in which any organization will engage. These should not be included in the organization's list of activities. The list should include only those activities associated with the organization's products and services (including membership) that are offered to members. Let's do an exercise to examine these concepts.

Exercise 5.1

Develop a list of five major activities of the organization and their net contribution to the organization's bottom line. After you have developed a list, identify the net revenue (i.e., total revenue minus total expense including, if available, staff and overhead allocations) of each activity. Many organizations have accounting systems that allow them to track costs by project. If such a system is not available to you, estimate costs for each project.

Many organizations only account for direct income and expenses but it is not uncommon to find that 40%–50% of an association's total budget is spent on staff wages and benefits. Failing to include such costs is a core mistake that will lead to a gross underestimate of the true cost of an activity. If the organization does not track staff costs via timesheets or some other method, we suggest that management, working with the staff directly involved, estimate the percent of time a staff member spends on each activity in order that the organization can arrive at an educated estimate of labor costs.

In addition to identifying costs, it is important to gather information about how much each product or service is used. Some products and services are included in members' dues (e.g., membership directories, information on the web). It will be important to identify ways to measure use. In some cases, associations collect data via surveys regarding use. Other products and services are offered for an additional fee. These will be easy to count, but use does not necessarily mean satisfaction. Continued use serves as a proxy to satisfaction, but it is better to have collected, whenever possible, user satisfaction data. Conducting a quantitative member needs assessment survey measuring importance and satisfaction with a gap analysis is the best way to accurately measure these product elements over time.

MANAGING THE ACTIVITY PORTFOLIO

One of the things we have learned about many remarkable associations is that they effectively align their products and services with their vision and mission. We will use the catalogue of your organization's major activities to determine the degree of alignment with your mission, objectives, and member needs. Consider the activity alignment matrix in Figure 5.1. The vertical axis defines the net gain or loss of each organizational activity. That part is relatively straightforward. We also want to plot the relative alignment of each activity. We suggest that you use a simple 10-point scale as shown. Taking into account the data you have collected on member use and satisfaction, as well as considering your organization's mission, objectives, and proposed strategies, how well does each activity align with those factors when considered collectively? An activity that is not mission related, does not address any of your objectives or strategies, and is not used by most members would receive a low score (1-2). On the other hand, an activity that is closely tied to your mission, objectives, and one or more of your strategies, and is used and liked by many members, would receive a high score (9-10).

Exercise 5.2

Assign an "alignment score" to each activity you listed in Exercise 5.1 Use a scale of 0-10, with 0 representing a total absence of alignment and 10 representing complete alignment. The decision of which activities should continue and which should remain is, ultimately, a subjective one. The purpose here is not to remove subjectivity, but rather to use a set of criteria that individuals within the organization agree to employ so as to reduce subjectivity. We suggest that senior staff within the organization, working as a team, first assign a proposed alignment score for each activity. These scores should then be presented to the board for their discussion and agreement.

Exercise 5.3

Once you have net revenue (positive or negative) and the alignment score for each activity, plot them on a chart similar to Figure 5.1. Now the organization is ready to make decisions on these activities based on where they appear on the chart.

QUADRANT ANALYSIS

Figure 5.1 depicts the relationship between an activity's net revenue and its organizational alignment. The horizontal line for alignment converges with the vertical line for net revenue at the midpoint for each axis ($0 for revenue and an alignment score of 5). The convergence of the net revenue and alignment axes results in four quadrants: 1) high net revenue, low alignment (Money Chasers); 2) high net revenue, high alignment (Sweet Spot); 3) low net revenue/high alignment (Sleepers); and 4) low net revenue/low alignment (Resource Drainers). Let's discuss them separately.

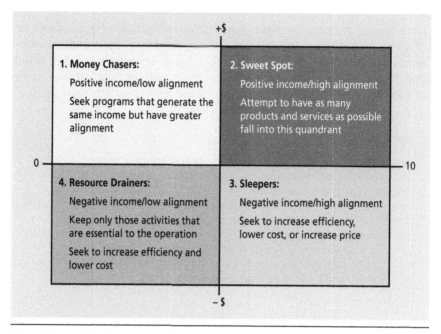

Figure 5.1   Activity alignment matrix.

Quadrant 1: Money Chasers

Activities in this quadrant are producing revenue for the organization; however, the activity is not driven by the organization's mission or it is not in alignment with its objectives or strategies. Some would ask: If the activity is making money for the organization, why should we be concerned?

As we stated earlier, great organizations are mission driven, not money driven. In our study of *7 Measures,* we found that one organization decided to not participate in an affinity credit card program.[23] To them, the reason for not doing so was simple: they were not in the credit card business. They made a conscious decision to focus on generating revenue from those activities that were closely aligned with their purpose. Their counterpart in the study, a good organization, found itself operating in the red for two consecutive years. The organization learned that it could generate revenue by receiving grants from the federal government to provide services overseas. After successfully obtaining grants, they moved into the black. A success story, right?

Wrong! The problem was that the organization was an American association composed of American members. The members asked, "Why are you providing all these services overseas and forgetting about us?" The leadership's response was, "Our members just don't get it. They don't understand that we need this money to survive." The leadership was right about one thing…the members didn't understand. As a result, membership began to drop. The organization was losing money. Rather than focusing on the conditions that resulted in financial loss, the leaders focused on money. They arrived at a short-term solution to their money problem, but in doing so they forgot their mission. The result was a loss of members the organization was initially formed to serve.

We are not suggesting that the organization eliminate all the activities in this quadrant. Indeed, there may be programs that require little organizational resources and generate significant revenue. For example, many organizations have affinity programs (e.g., credit card programs, endorsement programs) that require very little staff effort and result in income that can be used to support other mission-related programs. On the other hand, many organizations engage in activities that produce revenue but also require substantial organizational resources and effort (e.g., some grants). Therefore, we suggest that organizations carefully consider the wisdom of engaging in activity outside of their mission and, when advisable, attempt to systematically replace those revenue-generating activities with revenue-generating activities that will produce the same financial result but be more aligned with the organization's purpose. We see this often with organizations that have foundations. Certainly, foundations want to raise money. But chasing money is not a successful strategy in the long run. Your activities should be determined by your agenda, not by an outside source. You should produce those things that bring value to the members (or beneficiaries) you aim to serve.

Quadrant 2: The Sweet Spot

Items in this quadrant show a positive return on investment and high alignment with the organization's mission, objectives, and strategies. It's the perfect place to be. The organization should review the programs and services in the other three quadrants with the goal of altering as many as possible so that future performance will place them in this quadrant.

Quadrant 3: Sleepers

Quadrant 3 items show high alignment but a negative financial return. In truth, there will always be some items that belong here. In carrying out its mission, an association will identify certain programs that are highly aligned with its mission, objectives, and strategies but do not produce positive revenue. The problem with many associations is that they misunderstand their non-profit status and assume that many, if not most, of their projects should fall into this category. As we have stated before, non-profit is a *tax status*, not a *performance status*. Associations, like their for-profit counterparts, cannot survive for very long with a negative bottom line.

Organizations that provided highly needed services at a loss should do so knowingly—and they should know where the money will come from to pay for these services. Membership, for example, is a product. When an association solicits members, it offers a set of programs and services (benefits) in return for member dues. Wise associations understand the cost of those benefits and ensure that the revenue from dues is sufficient to pay for those services. Either that, or they purposely identify other revenue sources (for example, net meeting revenue) to pay for those services. They avoid the trap of continually adding "benefits" to membership that serve only to drive up the cost, without increasing membership value and thus, membership revenue.

Successful organizations understand there is no such thing as "free." Many boards decide to offer certain products and services free to members. Of course those services are not free; they have a cost. That cost must be paid either from member dues or another source. The board must act responsibly and judiciously in understanding what products and services it can subsidize with dues or other revenue.

As organizations review this list, then, we suggest they carefully consider the following questions about each item in this quadrant:

1. Is it proper to cover the cost of this item from dues revenue or from another revenue source within the association?

2. Can we take steps to reduce the cost of the item without detracting from its perceived value?

3. Related to question 2, are we producing the item in the most effective and efficient way?

4. Could we charge a price that would either pay for the item or at least reduce the financial loss?

Quadrant 4: Resource Drainers

Every association has certain products that show a financial loss and that either are not aligned with the organization's mission or do not generate much interest among members. Our study showed that remarkable associations that were faced with such programs did not hesitate to jettison them. By definition, products in this quadrant are serving no purpose, either financially or programmatically. Unless they are discontinued or altered in some way to increase their performance, they will continue to drain the resources and health of the organization.

When reviewing programs in this area, some managers and board members will argue that because the association is a non-profit organization, it will have some programs that serve only a limited few. To eliminate such programs, they further argue, would be a disservice to those members (although few in number) and not in keeping with the organization's mission. It is entirely possible that an organization might have a program that is very much in keeping with its mission but one that only a few members use and value. To be sure, those few who use it may even love it. As we noted, however, the program is not free. If organizational leaders wish to continue such a program, they must ask whether it is appropriate to require the majority of members to subsidize the cost of this program (via their dues payments) for the benefit of the few members who use the product or service. The answer may be yes. We suggest, however, that this answer should be the exception rather than the rule. As much as possible, products in this area should be eliminated or at least be paid for by the members who want them!

SUMMARY

Most organizations are not lacking in good mission-oriented ideas. The key question is whether these ideas have the potential for creating member value and assisting in revenue production. Further, most organizations do not have the resources to effectively implement all the good mission-oriented ideas available to them. Therefore, the challenge is to determine, through a disciplined process, which of the many ideas available best fit the organization's financial and human resources *and* members' desires. To accomplish this task we have presented a systematic process for:

1. Developing an organizational portfolio: a list of all the major products, services, and projects of the organization

2. Identifying the net revenue of each activity

3. Assigning an alignment score to each activity based on the degree to which the activity matches the organization's mission, objectives, strategic initiatives, and members' wants

4. Plotting each activity's position on the Activity Alignment Matrix based on its net revenue contribution and alignment score

5. Deciding whether to continue, eliminate, or alter an activity based on its position on the matrix and overall value to the association

These questions, when viewed with the information above, will ensure you are focused on the appropriate results in managing your portfolio of activities.

BALDRIGE CRITERIA
SUGGESTIONS AND QUESTIONS

As you manage your portfolio of products and services, the Baldrige Criteria for Performance Excellence asks you to consider important questions when creating your operational plan. How does your product line management focus address the following areas:

- Are you focusing on mission-oriented results and creating value for your constituents?

- Do you have a management process with feedback as outlined above to identify key value benefits and services?

- Are you using appropriate qualitative and quantitative research with your members and other constituents to identify new value offerings?

- How do your value programs, products, and services compare to your competition's offerings?

These questions, when viewed with the information above, will ensure you are focused on the appropriate results in managing your portfolio of activities.

6

Creating the Right Structure for Organizational and Human Performance

OPS MODEL

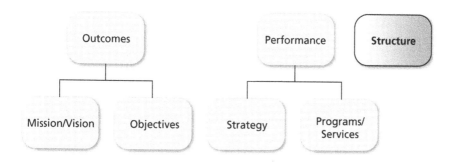

PRE-ASSESSMENT

Prior to beginning this chapter, answer each of the questions below, marking the corresponding box for yes, no, or don't know (DK). If you answer "yes" to all of the questions, we suggest you might want to quickly review this chapter and move to the next chapter. If you answer "no" to any of the questions, the material in this chapter will be helpful to your organization in providing remedies.

Question	YES	NO	DK
Are the objectives of functional units (departments, committees, divisions, and so on) aligned with the overall objectives of the organization?	☐	☐	☐
Are individuals in the organization assigned performance objectives consistent with those of functional units (departments, committees, divisions, etc.) of which they are members as well as the overall objectives of the organization?	☐	☐	☐
Is performance evaluated at organizational, functional unit, and individual levels?	☐	☐	☐
Are staff members' pay increases directly related to measures of staff performance?	☐	☐	☐
Do all performers (both staff and volunteers) have clearly written job descriptions?	☐	☐	☐
Do individual performers as well as members of groups (committees, task forces, departments, etc.) understand what is expected of them and how success will be measured?	☐	☐	☐
Do individuals and members of functional units understand how their performance affects not only the achievement of organizational objectives, but also how their performance affects the performance of other individuals and units within the organization?	☐	☐	☐
When failure occurs, does it undergo proper analysis in order to better understand what *not* to repeat?	☐	☐	☐

CHAPTER OVERVIEW

Successful organizations focus on clear outcomes, engage in performance that will lead to those outcomes, and ensure structures and resources are in place to support desired performance. We have referred to these three key elements as OPS: Outcomes, Performance, and Structure. The previous chapters have focused on specifying outcomes and outlining the performance required to achieve those outcomes. The succeeding chapters will focus on structure.

The research literature in Human Performance Improvement (HPI) tells us that a significant percentage of performance problems in the workplace are the result of a faulty structure, not a faulty performer.[24,25,26] The lesson for us, then, is that when we fail to get the performance we want, we should first look for problems within the organizational structure rather than blame people within the organization. This chapter will focus on how to create a structure to best facilitate performance.

Before getting too deeply into specifics, it is important to be clear about terminology. As with all disciplines, terminology used within a discipline often differs in meaning from the same terms as they are used in everyday language. *Credit,* for example, has a very different meaning to an accountant than it does to the average person. Our purpose in this chapter is not to present an academic lesson in human performance improvement. Rather, we will translate lessons learned in HPI to practical issues organizations face. Before we can do that, however, we need to explain how HPI uses certain terms and, more importantly, the concepts associated with those definitions.

Let's begin with the basic concept of performance. To the layperson, "performance" and "behavior" are synonymous. To the HPI professional these terms are fundamentally different. More importantly, those differences have important practical implications. Behavior is simply activity. Walking, talking, writing, reading—are all behaviors. Performance, on the other hand, refers to the outcomes or the effects of the behavior.[27,28] Running a mile in less than four minutes, speaking in a way that convinces others to act, and producing a brochure that leads to increased membership are all statements of performance.

Why does the difference matter? It matters because all organizations, or more accurately, all *people* within in an organization, engage in behavior; however, not all behavior leads to an intended outcome. Focusing on hard work and good intentions and failing to measure the effects of that hard work ultimately leads to organizational failure. At the end of the day, if the organization is not producing what it intends to produce, all the hard work in the world won't save it from failure. Noted author Stephen Covey illustrates this point well when he describes a person who, without a clear mission and purpose, puts forth great effort climbing a ladder leaning against a tall building. When he arrives at the top he discovers he has placed the ladder against the wrong wall. Behavior refers to climbing a ladder; performance refers to getting to the top of the right building.

Too often organizations focus on behavior—or even the "intent" behind the behavior—without defining the desired effect of the behavior and measuring whether that effect was achieved. Our discussion will focus on performance as we have defined it here.

Secondly, when we are discussing organizational performance, we are referring to the performance of people within the organization. Such performance can be measured at the organizational level: the outcomes of the collective performance of the individuals with the organization, the performance of functional units within the organization (the collective performance of individuals within departments, divisions, committees, and so on), and individual performance. All are important areas of focus and each will be discussed in its proper context.

Thirdly, associations and other non-profits have a challenge not typically faced by for-profit organizations: the workforce of non-profits is composed of both paid and unpaid staff (volunteers). When discussing ways to manage performance, we will address the different approaches needed for these two groups within a non-profit.

ORGANIZATIONAL PERFORMANCE

The best sources for descriptions of organizational performance are the objectives we described in Chapter 2. The organization wishes to increase non-dues revenue by x or increase membership by y. It is important, as we discussed in Chapter 3, to outline what people are going to do to achieve those objectives both at the functional unit level and at the individual level. By documenting both behavior and effect we measure performance. For example, when the organization did x, it resulted in organization performance at the desired level. Or perhaps the organization underperformed. The latter is not a statement of failure. By paying attention to behavior *and* its effect, we are in a position to learn what to repeat and what *not* to repeat. Failure to perform is only a problem in an organization when the failure is not recognized and repetition leads to more failure. As the Baldrige Criteria for Performance Excellence point out over and over, any organizational failure is an "opportunity for improvement." When an organization learns from its mistakes, it creates success from failure and ensures a better future.

What should be clear from this discussion is that simply focusing on behavior—activity—is not an acceptable surrogate for measuring performance. Many boards spend a great amount of time gathering and listening to activity reports (e.g., "The Meetings Committee put on an educational program," …"The Membership Committee sent a brochure to 300 potential members,"… "The Public Relations Committee developed a publication that reached 100,000 people"). Unless the board goes to the extra step of assessing the actual effects of those efforts against the standards that were set (i.e., objectives), such activity reports are of little value.

Let's look at a practical example. Many on association boards believe it is vitally important to have a website. When asked why a website is needed, some board members fall into the trap of circular reasoning: "We need a website. Currently, we don't have one. Therefore, we need to develop one." The board then receives progress reports and believes it has achieved organizational success when the website is up and running, particularly if the board likes the design. By our definition, the board is focused on behavior, not performance.

A performance-based approach might look something like this: We need to increase member retention by 3%. Members report that paying dues from a mailer they receive is cumbersome and causes them to delay renewing. They would be more likely to pay their dues if they could do so online. The organization, therefore, must develop that capability on the website. Effectiveness (i.e., organizational performance) would be measured in terms of the number of members who renewed via the website as well as overall retention rates. Simply providing members the capability to renew their dues on a website would not be considered success; that is an activity. If the activity leads to reduced attrition (performance), then we can consider the performance a success.

FUNCTIONAL UNIT PERFORMANCE

Effective organizations ensure that each sub-unit contributes to the intended outcomes of the organization as a whole. Not only is it important for each unit to understand how its performance relates to the organization's intended outcomes, but units must also understand how their performance affects the work of other units.[29]

Let's consider some examples. Assume an organization seeks to increase membership at its annual meeting by 4%. The education department and related committees must insure the content of the meeting is aimed at addressing documented needs. They must also ensure that the number of sessions offered and the scheduling of those sessions are feasible given the arrangements with the hotel or convention center. The finance department can cause problems for the meetings department if it aggressively purses payment of registration fees. Members who feel harassed may cancel their meeting registration... as well as their membership. So, in short, all units must understand not only how their performance affects the organization as a whole but also how their performance affects the performance of the other units.

INDIVIDUAL PERFORMANCE

When evaluating individuals, organizations often engage in "behavior review"—or worse, "trait" review—rather than performance review. As we have noted, the organization should be concerned with the effects of the behavior rather than simply looking at the behavior itself. To the degree possible, all staff in the organization should be asked to achieve performance goals. The evaluation should focus not on how hard they worked, but on what affect their behavior had on helping the organization achieve its strategic objectives.

We are not arguing that this should be the *only* focus of evaluation. If employees achieve results at the expense of others in the organization or engage in unacceptable behavior in carrying out their duties, this must be accounted for as well. However, most organizations are not equipped to measure, let alone alter, basic personality traits. Attempting to evaluate whether a staff member was "friendly," a "team player," or "responsible" is not easily measurable and, in most cases, does not provide the staff member or the organization with useful information.

When attempting to evaluate "how" someone performed his or her job (aside from the results they produced), the organization is well advised to measure behavior. Examples of measurement might include:

1. Keeps supervisor well informed
2. Maintains confidences
4. Is open to constructive feedback
5. Provides constructive feedback
7. Ensures the ideas of others are heard

Such scales are referred to as *behaviorally anchored scales* because they attempt to measure behavior as opposed to emotions or attitudes.[30] These scales become stronger with the use of specific examples, either positive or negative, that illustrate how employees were evaluated. Numerous sources for such scales can be found in performance evaluation literature online and elsewhere. One of the authors has developed a behaviorally anchored scale for assessing managerial performance. That form appears in Figure 6.1 later in this chapter.

Having described the three levels performance—organizational, functional unit, and individual—we now discuss how organizational structure and policy can be used to enhance performance. Performance is a function of 1) the conditions under which the performance occurs, 2) the knowledge, skills, and abilities (KSAs) of the performers, and 3) the consequences of the performers' actions. Let's begin with conditions.

MANAGING CONDITIONS

One of the single most important factors contributing to job stress—and nonperformance—is role ambiguity.[31] Many workers are unclear about what is expected of them. So, the first step to achieve the proper performance is to specify it. We have discussed the importance of SMART (specific, measurable, achievable, relevant, timely) objectives. As we have noted, those objectives should be clearly communicated to all staff and volunteers. Moreover, all functional units (committees, departments, task forces, and so on) should have clearly specified objectives they are to achieve, consistent with the organization's objectives. Likewise, individuals should have corresponding objectives they are to achieve. Also, each unit and performer within the unit should know what they are to produce: a program, a policy, a set of recommendations, a background paper, and so on. In other words, everyone should be clear on the "deliverable" they are to produce. If they are to work within a set of given parameters (a budget, policy guidelines, and so on), those should be made clear. The more clear expectations are made, the more likely they are to be met.

Often, boards and managers confuse means with ends. If an organization wishes to hold a functional unit or an individual accountable for results, it should not specify the means as well as the ends.

Consider a common example. The board has assigned the CEO with the objective of increasing attendance at its annual meeting by 3% next year. It also has told the CEO that the board must approve the site of the meeting. It is well known that meeting location is a critical factor affecting meeting attendance. If the board wishes to prescribe the means, it (not the CEO) must also be accountable for the ends. A more proper role for the board is to specify the outcome (3% increase in attendance and excess revenue of $400,000) and then allow the CEO and assigned volunteers to use whatever means they deem proper to achieve those ends within limits prescribed by the board.

Not all individuals within an organization will be (or should be) accountable for results. Consider a popular hamburger chain. The organization seeks to provide the customer with a consistent product in a fast and inexpensive manner. It does not instruct the staff to use whatever means they wish to accomplish the task. Rather, the staff is directed to follow fairly rigid rules and procedures to deliver the product. In this case, staff members are held accountable for complying with those rules and procedures, not with the results of those procedures.[32]

Many staff within an organization will be given policies and procedures to follow. They should be held accountable for complying with them. Those developing the policies and procedures should be held accountable for the results produced when those policies and procedures are followed.

Staff and volunteers should also have clearly written job descriptions detailing the duties and responsibilities associated with the positions they hold. Committees and task forces should be given clear charges detailing what they are to deliver and when. For example, the board of an association directed its membership committee to "increase member awareness of the value of membership." If you were a member of the committee, would you know what the board wanted you to produce? How would you know you had succeeded in completing the assignment? A more clear charge to the committee might be: "Develop written strategies to increase the number of new members and decrease member attrition." The board of another association directed its meeting committee to develop a two-day conference on a specific topic. This directive makes sense *if* the board has correctly identified a member need associated with the topic and has further determined that a two-day course is the proper solution to that need. A more appropriate charge might be as follows: "Develop and implement educational programs addressing documented needs and producing net revenue of $50,000 collectively."

Some tasks within an organization are performed routinely while other tasks are performed less frequently. The less frequently a task is performed, the more opportunity there will be for errors in performance. Job aides are useful tools in such cases.[33] Years ago, cashiers at grocery stores entered the price of each item on a cash register. The cashier then accepted payment and, in most cases, had to figure out how much change to give back to the customer. Today, cashiers merely scan items. They then enter the amount of the payment received and the computer tells the cashier how much money to return to the customer. A job aid is a tool that provides information or instructions on how to complete a task in a quick and easy manner. A staff phone directory is another simple example. Rather than expecting staff to recall each person's phone number, a directory is provided. Nearly all software applications have a "help" feature, a job aid that provides instructions on how to solve a problem. Other examples include pre-flight checklists for pilots, spell check in Word, and instruction cards attached to a copier. Job aids also provide a relatively inexpensive alternative to training in many cases where the task involves routine procedures

Many volunteer board members have little to no knowledge of parliamentary procedure. To be sure, many associations invest time and resources providing annual training on parliamentary procedure for board members. Given that for most volunteers parliamentary procedure is foreign to their day jobs, and given further that most boards typically meet only three to four times per year, putting forth such a training effort may not produce the best results. Recognizing this, many associations provide their members with a job aid in the form of a table listing the most common parliamentary actions, the manner in which a person initiates those actions, and the manner in which such actions are decided (e.g., no vote, simple majority, super majority, and so on).

Exercise 6.1

Identify non-routine tasks or tasks performed infrequently that might be enhanced with a job aid. Identify the form and content of the job aid(s) for each task.

Current task that has potential to be replaced with a job aid.	What would the form of the job aid be (a chart, algorithm, a list, etc.)?	What content would the job aid contain?
Meeting planner must remember what details to discuss with the hotel	Checklist	Critical details associated with a successful meeting

Feedback is critically important to effective performance. In fact, the Baldrige Criteria continually emphasize the importance of feedback to organizational learning. Did the performance lead to the desired outcome? If not, why not? What can be learned from our mistakes? Performance problems are the result of a lack of tools, competence, or motivation. Competence refers to the knowledge, skills, and abilities (KSAs) needed to get the job done. As Jim Collins has noted, it involves having the right people on the bus and getting the wrong people off the bus. Selection of the right people for the job is critical. Does each performer have the required KSAs? If not, can we get those who do? If we cannot, then we probably should not undertake the activity. Can we get the people who have the KSAs they need via information sources or training?

Exercise 6.2

Select one of the strategies you developed in Exercise 3.2 in Chapter 3 and complete the following table in order to identify KSAs your organization needs, which of those KSAs it has, and which KSAs it needs to acquire.

Strategy:

_____

_____

KSAs required (e.g., marketing skills, specific content knowledge, data analysis skills, etc.)	KSA exists within the organization	For KSAs checked "no," describe how KSA will be acquired (e.g., training, outsourcing, etc.)
	☐ Yes ☐ No	
	☐ Yes ☐ No	
	☐ Yes ☐ No	

MANAGING CONSEQUENCES

Some individuals or teams have the competence but fail to perform. In such cases it is important to look at the consequences of their efforts. What happened as a result of their efforts or lack of effort? Robert Mager, an early pioneer in HPI, suggests that when managers identify a performance problem caused by a lack of motivation (as opposed to a lack of training or practice), the manager should ask four important questions:[34]

1. Is performance punishing? What is rewarding for some is punishing for others. Whether something is rewarding or punishing is determined by its effect on performance. A consequence is rewarding if it increases performance; it is punishing if it decreases performance. If performance declines, the consequences were, by definition, punishing. If you are noticing a decline in an individual's or a group's performance, then look to what happens after the performance.

Consider this common example: "I don't understand," a supervisor bemoans. "John used to be so good at dealing with difficult members. He doesn't seem as happy now." Every time John handled a difficult member, he was assigned another. For him, good performance was punished. Another supervisor relates the following: "Sally used to be a great committee member. Whenever we needed something done, Sally was our 'go to' volunteer. Lately, she seems totally uninterested. She doesn't return emails for days and is late in completing assignments." In other words, Sally's "reward" for completing an activity was more work. Performance became punishing for Sally.

2. Is non-performance rewarding? If you find yourself saying, "If I want anything done right around here, I have to do it myself," you might discover that you are inadvertently rewarding non-performance. Some staff and members quickly learn that if they fall behind, someone else will pick up the slack and do it for them. Others learn that if they whine and complain, they can get out of doing jobs they don't like. They use statements such as, "Why do I always get the dirty jobs? Can't you find someone else to do that?" Rather than dealing with the unpleasant staff member, the manager finds it easier to give the job to someone else. In doing so, however, the manager is rewarding whining and complaining rather than getting the important work done.

3. Does performance matter? People who are habitually late for meetings have learned that nothing happens if they are late; there are no consequences. Committees fail to produce what they have been assigned. So what? Nothing happens. In fact, sometimes non-performance is rewarded; members are placed on another committee. This is why we have stressed having measurable outcomes. By measuring performance, you are making it matter. You are calling attention to performance—or the lack of it.

4. Are there obstacles to performance? The person or group may have the KSAs and may be motivated, but may not have time to complete the assignment. When performance is not occurring, supervisors need to ask: Does the person (group) assigned have too much to do? Do they have sufficient budget and other resources? Are they awaiting decisions or approvals from others? Do they have all the information they need?

Exercise 6.3

Let's practice analyzing a performance problem. Think of a person (or group) who reports to you or works with you and who is posing a performance problem. The purpose of this exercise is to analyze the problem and develop an action plan. Remember, a problem is a critical difference between *what should be* and *what is*. The first step is to make sure that a problem does, in fact, exist. It's important to be sure the organization is focusing on a problem, not on a symptom of a problem. The following steps are based on Robert Mager's algorithm for analyzing performance problems:

1. Define what the person (group) should do. (The description of the desired performance should state an observable behavior.)

2. Next, describe the actual performance you have observed.

3. Is there a critical difference between what should be and what is? (A critical difference is a difference you cannot live with or accept.)

   a. ☐ Yes, and I cannot live with the difference.

   b. ☐ No, there is no difference (or the difference is one I can live with).

   If you answered "no" to question 3, you can go get a cup of coffee and learn to be more tolerant of the person in question. If you answered "yes" to question 3, go to the next question.

4. When the person fails to perform, is there a consequence for not performing? Does anything happen?

   a. ☐ Yes

   b. ☐ No

   If you answered "no" to question 4, make performance matter. Provide a positive consequence for proper performance. If you answered, "yes," go to the next question.

5. Did the person perform at an acceptable level in the past and has that person now stopped performing at the desired level?

   a. ☐ Yes

   b. ☐ No

Exercise 6.3 *(continued)*

If you answered "yes" to question 5, whatever followed the desired performance in the past was viewed as punishing by the performer (regardless of how you or others viewed it). In the future, ensure that positive consequences (as viewed by the performer) follow. If you answered "no" to the question 5, the performer is being rewarded for non-performance. If you have gotten to this point in the process, it means that the person is not performing at the desired level and also that there is a consequence for not performing. By definition, whatever that consequence is, the person views it as rewarding. The consequence must be removed. A person should only receive a positive consequence (as defined by the performer) when he/she performs at the desired level.

The means for adding or removing a consequence will be covered in the next chapter on providing feedback.

PAY FOR PERFORMANCE

One of the single most important factors to increased performance is pay. Pay for performance has been shown to significantly increase productivity in some work settings.[35,36,37] In order for pay for performance to be effective, the following conditions must be present:[38]

1. The rules of the pay-for-performance program must be clear.

2. The rules must be seen as both reasonable and achievable.

3. The performer must believe that the pay-for-performance program will be sufficiently funded.

4. The performer must believe that if the conditions are met, he/she will actually be paid.

Certainly people do not work solely for money. Some work environments are so oppressive that no amount of money makes working in them worthwhile for some employees. However, the reverse is also true. A highly pleasant work environment will not always be sufficient to attract or retain some members if the pay is not competitive. Employees must view the pay they receive as commensurate with the contributions they make to the organization as a result of their performance. While sufficient pay does not guarantee sufficient performance, insufficient pay is almost always associated with insufficient performance. One must meet the minimum threshold and then add other benefits such as more responsibility, recognition, travel to seminars, and so on.

Pay-for-performance plans typically guarantee a base salary for all performers who meet minimum performance standards. Those exceeding the standards earn additional pay based on a clearly described formula. This additional incentive pay is said to be "at risk." In other words, unlike base pay, this portion of a person's compensation is directly tied to the achievement of goals set in advance. Failure to achieve these goals results in a failure to receive either all or a portion of the at-risk amount. The research on pay for performance demonstrates that the amount of salary at risk need not be great. Assuming the base pay is at a competitive level, at-risk pay as low as 3% of a person's base pay has been demonstrated to be effective. Moreover, there is a point of diminishing returns. Those who receive 20% pay at risk typically perform no better than those who have 10% of their pay at risk.[39] Non-profits designing incentive pay systems must also guard against issues of inurement (i.e., financial benefit to individuals). Certainly paying for doing a job is not considered inurement; however, excessive pay is. As long as a person's total compensation is reasonable (i.e., within the range of compensation of others in similar positions with similar responsibilities), then inurement should not be an issue. Organizations seeking to establish pay-for-performance systems are wise to seek the advice of persons with expertise in compensation systems as well as accounting and legal professionals with expertise in the area of compensation for non-profits.

Incentive plans

One of the authors established an incentive compensation system when he served as COO of a medical specialty society. At that time, the association had an expense budget of $15,000,000 and a staff of 100. There were 11 pay grades and each pay grade had a published minimum, mid-point, and maximum for salary. The incentive compensation plan that was presented to and approved by the board operated as follows:

1. Prior to the beginning of the fiscal year, the board established a specific amount of excess revenue (profit) it wished to achieve at the end of the fiscal year (e.g., $150,000).

2. At the end of the fiscal year, the target for profit was subtracted from the actual amount.

3. For every dollar in excess of the target, 60% was retained in member equity, and 40% was placed in a bonus pool.

Incentive plans *(continued)*

4. If sufficient funds were available in the bonus pool to make incentives meaningful (at least 1% of a performer's base salary), bonus funds were distributed to staff based on their performance review, as follows:

   a. Competent performers (i.e., those achieving but not exceeding performance standards) received no bonus.

   b. Commendable performers (those exceeding performance standards by a specified amount) received up to 5% of their salary as a bonus.

   c. Outstanding performers (those exceeding performance standards by a specified amount that was higher than the commendable level) received up to 10% of their salary as a bonus.

   d. The amount of the percentage for commendable and outstanding performance was determined by the amount in the bonus pool. Commendable performers received x% and outstanding performers received 2 times x% up to the limits set for each level (5% and 10%, respectively).

   e. Bonus payments were considered one-time payments and did not accrue to a staff member's base salary.

If performance incentives are not carefully thought out, unintended consequences can occur.[40] For example, an emergency nurse may receive incentive pay based upon how quickly he/she sees a patient. Unless incentives are also based on how quickly patients are *appropriately* discharged from the emergency department as well as on how satisfied patients are with the services they receive, the emergency department might find that patients have been quickly seen by a nurse and then had their definitive care delayed.

Exercise 6.4

Table 6.1 contains elements essential to an effective compensation system. Complete the table by indicating whether your organization's compensation system contains these elements. If an element is not present, use the comments section to record notes for taking corrective action.

Element	Present in your organization's system?	Comments on corrective action
1. Performance goals are specific and measurable.	☐ Yes ☐ No	
2. The rules governing the compensation system are clear and specific.	☐ Yes ☐ No	
3. The pay for performance occurs within a few weeks of the performance evaluation.	☐ Yes ☐ No	
4. Performers are paid in accordance with the rules of the compensation system.	☐ Yes ☐ No	
5. Performers have formal recourse for addressing disagreements with their evaluation.	☐ Yes ☐ No	
6. Both monetary and nonmonetary incentives are made contingent upon proper performance.	☐ Yes ☐ No	
7. Alignment exists between the objectives of the organization, its business units, and the objectives of the individuals working in those units.	☐ Yes ☐ No	

Table 6.1 Elements of an effective compensation system.

In summary, the success of any incentive compensation or pay-for-performance plan depends heavily on the degree to which it helps employees understand how their individual performance relates to organization, department, or group goals. One study revealed that only 31% of the companies surveyed believed that employees' goals are aligned with those of the organization.

So far, we have been discussing how to manage the consequences of performers via pay. However, many performers in an association are volunteers who receive no pay, at least in the traditional sense. Nonetheless, the organization can, and should, monitor the performance of volunteers and seek to influence positive performance through the proper use of incentives.

We have emphasized that an "incentive" is defined by how it affects performance. If desired performance increases, the consequence is a positive incentive; if performance decreases, the consequence is a punisher. Remember these definitions derive from the viewpoint of the performer, *not* the organization. Often leaders will lament that volunteers should *want* to participate. The fact is, volunteers will participate *if* they view participation as resulting in pleasing consequences. Suggestions for non-monetary incentives for both staff and volunteers appear in Table 6.2.

Many organizations do not get desired performance from member volunteers because they do not make the attainment of desirable incentives contingent on desirable performance. Volunteers' performance is often ignored (no consequence) or volunteers receive incentives *despite* poor performance. Concerning the latter, associations are replete with examples of poorly performing volunteers who are advanced to the next level to avoid a repeat of their bad performance at a previous level or to get them out of someone's hair. (The result, of course, is that they turn up in someone else's hair!)

Potential Non-Monetary Incentives for Volunteers		
Spouse travel benefits	Choice of project	Free lunch/dinner
Job enrichment	Off-site training	Flexible schedule
Committee assignments	Job title	Professional conference
Interaction with other members	Formal recognition of service	Opportunities for promotion
		Opportunities to dine in a convivial atmosphere with fellow members

Table 6.2 Non-monetary incentives.

The principles for managing volunteer performers are the same as for managing the performance of paid staff. The difference lies with the incentives provided. To review, those principles include:

1. Desired performance should be specified via written position descriptions for all leaders and for all committees and committee members.

2. Performance evaluations of all volunteers should be conducted by appropriate parties (board members should evaluate officers as well as each other). The president, board, and committee members should evaluate committee members. And the chair (president) should evaluate committee members. Staff can submit independent evaluations of volunteers to volunteer leaders in charge of those volunteers.

3. Decisions regarding advancement within the organization should be based on evaluation, as well as on the products, programs, and services produced.

SUMMARY

In this chapter, we have discussed the importance of aligning the objectives, resources, and budgets of the different parts of the organization with the overall objectives of the organization. Measurement of organizational and individual performance is essential to success (see Figure 6.1 for an assessment form example). If performance does not matter, it will not occur. Therefore, rewards for individuals (both monetary and non-monetary) should be directly tied to their performance. The organization should report organizational and individual performance and analyze organizational and individual strategy execution.

XYZ Association

Supervisor Assessment

Name of staff member:_____

Staff's position title: _____

Name of evaluator: _____

Date: _____

Directions: Please read each competency statement and use the scale below to rate the degree to which you believe the competency statement is a true description of the staff member's behavior on the job. If you believe a competency statement is not relevant to the staff member's current position, place "NR" in the rating column.

Competency	Rating
1. Effectively plans and organizes projects impacting the work of others	
2. Maintains confidences	
3. Is open to constructive criticism	
4. Offers constructive criticism	
5. Communicates ideas effectively	
6. Is respected by coworkers	
7. Identifies problems in a timely fashion and develops effective solutions	
8. Takes appropriate initiative	
9. Properly delegates to others	
10. Listens well to others	
11. Appropriately relays progress, obstacles, and opportunities	
12. Manages conflict appropriately	

Assessment Scale

5: Occurs without exception

4: Usually occurs

3: Occurs infrequently

1: Occurs seldom if ever

NR: Not relevant

Figure 6.1 Assessment of managerial competencies.

BALDRIGE CRITERIA
SUGGESTIONS AND QUESTIONS

In an effort to improve individual and organizational performance, the Baldrige Criteria for Performance Excellence asks you to consider the following questions when developing your structure, evaluating key factors of performance, and developing performance evaluation criteria:

- How do you select, collect, align, and integrate data and information for tracking organizational performance?

- What are your key organizational performance measures, including key short-term and long-term financial criteria, and how are they integrated into the fabric of your organizational structure?

- How do you use these data and information to support organizational decision making and innovation?

- In terms of organizational agility, how do you ensure your performance measurement system is able to respond to rapid or unexpected organizational change?

- How do you use individual and organizational reviews to assess organizational success and progress towards accomplishing strategic goals and objectives?

The answers to these questions will ensure that your performance evaluation system and structure are moving the organization toward its stated vision and mission.

7

Ensuring Proper and Effective Feedback

OPS MODEL

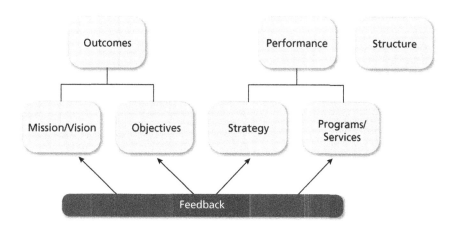

PRE-ASSESSMENT

Prior to beginning this chapter, answer each of the questions below, marking the corresponding box for yes, no, or don't know (DK). If you answer "yes" to all of the questions, we suggest you might want to quickly review this chapter and move to the next chapter. If you answer "no" to any of the questions, the material in this chapter will be helpful to your organization in correcting the situation.

Question	YES	NO	DK
Is performance evaluated at organizational, functional unit, and individual levels?	☐	☐	☐
Are data-based objective feedback consistently used to improve performance?	☐	☐	☐
Are programs evaluated to determine if they are successfully meeting member needs?	☐	☐	☐
Are programs not meeting member needs either dropped or revised?	☐	☐	☐
Does the organization's leadership demonstrate an ability to redirect resources based on analysis of the environment?	☐	☐	☐
Are evaluation data used to modify organizational activities?	☐	☐	☐
Do staff and volunteers receive regular feedback about how the organization is performing?	☐	☐	☐
Do individuals share accountability for organizational results?	☐	☐	☐

CHAPTER OVERVIEW

As we have discussed, organizations are open systems; they receive information and make changes based on that information. Feedback encourages organizational learning by providing information designed to bring about change. The fact is, many organizations do not effectively use feedback, or they use feedback in such a way as to bring about unintended negative consequences. If feedback is to be useful, it must be specific, properly timed, and communicated in a way that is understood by the performer.

As we will see in this chapter, feedback achieves one of two purposes: to prove or to improve.[41] We use the word "or" because it is essential to separate the two. Organizations are not effective when they try to use information to both prove and improve at the same time. Recall that in the last chapter, we explained that performance is a behavior with an effect. The purpose of feedback is to increase the probability that the effect of the organization's behavior is the one intended. Just as performance occurs at the organizational, functional unit, and individual levels, so too does effective feedback. This chapter will focus on the purpose of feedback and effective methods for appropriately using it to achieve the organization's desired ends.

ELEMENTS OF EFFECTIVE FEEDBACK

As one HPI expert noted, "(f)eedback is information about behavior or its impact, that is 'fed-back' to an individual or the group, with the intention of influencing future performance."[42] In other words, organizations use information to increase either how well or how much a person performs. Feedback aimed at improving quality is referred to as *formative evaluation*. The organization seeks to form or shape behavior to achieve a desired standard. Feedback that is designed to prove an outcome occurred, and more importantly, to ensure that it happens again, is referred to as *summative evaluation*. Let's consider each separately.

SUMMATIVE EVALUATION

All of us have experienced, and many of us have dreaded, various forms of summative evaluation. Final exams, entrance exams, and annual performance reviews are but a few examples of summative evaluation. It occurs at the completion of a performance and is intended to verify whether the outcome was satisfactory. The intended user of summative information is typically not the performer as much as it is the person or entity who wishes to benefit from the performance. Feedback cannot alter the performance; what's done is done. What feedback can do is encourage more of the same performance or discourage the repetition of more performance like it. Both uses are important when properly applied.[43]

Unfortunately, many of us have not witnessed good examples of properly used feedback. All too often, feedback is provided in general terms (e.g., "that was not good enough... I'm not satisfied, go and try again"), and accompanied by negative assessments of the performer rather than the performance (*you* failed; that wasn't a smart move; I can't believe *you* did that; are *you* kidding me?).

When managers and supervisors see performance they don't want, their tendency is often to use punishment to discourage any future occurrence. Punishment does work, in that it often stops an undesired behavior. Though effective in stopping a behavior, punishment brings about undesirable consequences, including:

- *Inhibited initiative:* When told what *not* to do (and not told what to do instead), most people avoid any performance that might risk censure.

- *Avoidance:* If we find something unpleasant, most of us will do whatever we can to avoid placing ourselves in similar situations in the future.

- *Escape:* If we are unable to foresee and therefore avoid an unpleasant situation, we will try our best to get out of the situation in which we unhappily find ourselves.

- *Rebellion:* If we are unable to escape or avoid a punishing situation, we will find ways to push back, to thwart or stop those who put us in the situation in the first place. Few subordinates are foolish enough to openly rebel. They do not want their "pushing back" to be punished, so they engage in "passive-aggressive" behavior that appears compliant but is actually designed to undermine their supervisor.[44]

All of us are aware of bad examples of using feedback. Let's focus on effective ways to use summative information at the organizational, functional unit, and individual levels.

Summative Evaluation at the Organizational Level

Summative evaluation should be valid (that is, measure what it purports to measure). It should also be free of noise and distraction; it should have specific focus. Many organizations do not engage in effective summative evaluations because they have not specified their intent. Many organizations express intent with statements such as: We will be the premier organization in the industry; We will be the go-to organization for our members; or We will be the champions for the highest standards in the profession. All of these aspirations are laudable. However, in absence of any further specificity, they remain wishes.

As we have stressed throughout this book, organizational success begins with clearly stated SMART objectives. Most organizations use a three-year to five-year horizon to project outcomes. At the end of that time period, the senior staff and the leadership will review the data to determine whether those objectives are met. When the objectives have been stated in measureable terms, the data points will be straightforward. The board and senior managers will decide, based on the data, whether the objectives have been met, exceeded, or not met.

Many organizations, associations in particular, wrestle with what data management should provide the board. In recent years, a good deal of conversation has centered on "dashboards." The notion of a dashboard is to ensure that critical metrics receive prominent notice and are not lost in a myriad of data. Many understand and agree with the notion of a dashboard but still struggle with knowing what the dashboard should contain. Having five to six SMART objectives at the organizational level helps resolve this issue. The metrics developed for the SMART objectives are those that appear on the dashboard. If, for example, the organization seeks to gain new members and increase member retention, then these membership statistics should be included in the dashboard. Said simply, the dashboard for the organization should contain the data related to each of the five to six key organizational objectives.

Exercise 7.1

Creating a dashboard. If objectives are to be appropriately managed, they must be kept in front of everyone in the organization. On the other hand, if too much data are provided, leaders lose their focus. Review the SMART objectives you developed in Chapter 1 and a complete a dashboard for your organization (see Table 7.1).

List SMART objectives in the first column and the metrics to be used in the second column. The third column should contain the most current value of the metric. Based on the current value of the metric and the months remaining to work on the objective, record the best-forecasted value for the objective at the completion of the plan. Use the comments section to record factors that may be positively or negatively affecting the successful completion of the objective.

SMART objective	Metric(s)	Starting data point	Current data point	Projected data point	Comments

Table 7.1   SMART objectives dashboard.

When objectives have been met or exceeded, everyone is pleased. Smart organizations are learning organizations. When objectives are not met, smart organizations do not view that outcome as a failure, but as a learning opportunity.[45] They do not seek to punish and blame, but rather to learn what might be done differently in the future. A failure teaches smart organizations that the strategies they employed did not bring about the intended change. The organization now has better information on what strategies might work. Or, the leadership may decide that although the original objective seemed like a good idea, it now appears that the organization does not have the capacity to achieve the desired outcome. Alternatively, the organization may decide that the potential value of achieving the desired outcome is not worth the potential cost of implementing a revised strategy.

Faultfinding and blame serve no purpose. The plain truth is that not meeting the objective is no *one's* fault; everyone is accountable. The authors are not particularly fond of sports analogies, but one seems appropriate for this discussion. We have all witnessed a football team lose a game in the final minutes as the result of a fumble or interception. It is easy to blame the player who committed the turnover for the loss, but it's entirely inaccurate. The fact that the team was behind until the closing minutes of the game is the responsibility of the *all* the people involved with the team, all the players and the coaches. By reviewing all that went on in the game, the team can learn what factors led to the loss and can make decisions about how to change things in the future. Blaming and scapegoating are viewed as punishing and, as we now know, punishment leads to more failure, not increased success.

Feedback sometimes informs us as to what we might do differently. It can also inform us as to what we should stop perusing. Both authors would love to achieve the goal of being scratch golfers, but that is not going to happen in our lifetimes. Rather than pursuing the unattainable, we have learned to modify our expectations. This decision is not about giving up. It is about making rational, data-based decisions about what is feasible, within our own (i.e., organizational) capabilities, and affordable.

Remember that the purpose of summative evaluation is to increase (or decrease) the quantity of performance. It is most effective in achieving that purpose when it is provided as soon as possible at the completion of performance. Therefore, summative evaluation at the organizational level should be completed as close as possible to the completion date stated in the organizational objectives.

The format of organizational summative evaluation should be simple and straightforward. It should contain the results (what succeeded, what didn't) and conclusions (addressing such questions as: Was the outcome worth the effort? What surprises occurred in pursuit of the objective? What did we fail to find?). If the objective was not met, it will be important for the evaluators to mention whether the required resources were available and if not, what caused their absence. Also, were the strategies and tactics carried out as planned? If not, what modifications (or deletions) were made and why? Remember, the purpose of this analysis is not to place blame but rather to determine what went wrong and why, and to create organizational learning and feedback to aid future decisions.

Exercise 7.2

Analysis of failure at the organizational level. All successful organizations experience failure from time to time. The difference between successful organizations and mediocre ones is that successful organizations learn from their failures. Working with leaders of the organization, identify a major program that was judged unsuccessful and answer the following questions regarding that program:

1. Were the objectives of the program clearly understood by all involved? In other words, was it clear to all why the program was being offered, and what metrics would be used to measure success?

2. Was each person's role in the project clearly defined?

3. Was someone assigned to monitor the performance of those involved and provide positive or corrective feedback as needed?

4. Was the project carried out as planned?

5. Did those involved in the project have the resources they needed?

6. Did those involved in the project encounter barriers that made proper performance difficult or impossible?

7. Does the problem or need the program was designed to address still exist?

8. Can the program be modified or redesigned to address the problem or need?

9. Is the modification or redesign worth the benefit that might accrue to the stakeholders? Does it really address the systemic problem or merely a symptom of the problem?

Summative Evaluation at the Functional Unit Level

Summative evaluation at this level is very similar to that of the organizational level. As we discussed in the last chapter, functional units refer to staff departments or divisions as well as volunteer committees and task forces. The focus at this level is on the sub-objectives assigned to organizational units. Given that we are discussing systems—units working together to achieve what no unit can achieve on its own—it will be important for evaluators to discuss whether any unit had challenges in working with other units while carrying out its assignments.

Summative Evaluation at the Individual Level

As we have noted, the purpose of summative evaluation is to increase or decrease the frequency of behavior. Therefore, unlike summative evaluation at the organizational or functional unit level that occurs at the designated completion of a behavior, summative evaluation for individuals should occur at the completion of a behavior whenever it occurs. When performers handle an assignment or complete a task, they should receive feedback as soon as possible. The weaker (i.e., the less frequent) the behavior, the more frequent feedback is required. As a performer's experience increases, the frequency of feedback can decrease. It is not our purpose here to provide an in-depth lesson in psychology or training. But it is important to point out that research has long demonstrated that new learners who receive more frequent feedback learn faster those who do not.[46,47,48,49] As performance builds, the frequency of performance can be maintained with increasingly less feedback.

Some performance provides immediate natural feedback. For example, when we turn the light switch on correctly we receive immediate feedback—the lamp lights. Placing our hand on a hot surface provides immediate natural feedback; we learn that repeating the behavior is not a good idea. In many cases, however, particularly in organizations, the natural feedback is delayed. The effects of many harmful personal bad habits (smoking, eating an unhealthy diet, substance abuse, and so on) are not realized until months or in some cases years after the behavior has occurred. The same is true with performance in the organization. This is particularly true since, as we have noted, individual performance occurs within a system. One person, working alone, seldom can produce an outcome that is produced by several people working together harmoniously. Therefore, our feedback on individual performance most often addresses a person's compliance with a prescribed plan rather than the effect of the individual behavior.[50]

Too often, feedback of individual performance tends to lack specificity. Commonly heard statements in the workplace include: "good job"; "you missed the mark"; "what a dumb decision, I can't believe you did that"; "are you kidding me?"; "you are (or are not) being a team player"; "you are (or are not) thinking strategically"; "you can do better than that…" All these communicate that the supervisor was either happy or unhappy with the performance. However, in most cases it is unclear to the performer exactly what performance led to the feedback. If feedback is to be effective, it must be as specific as possible, particularly with novice performers: "Your report contained all the elements I was expecting"; "your report missed the following elements…"; "you listened to the member's concerns and took the proper course of action"; "you followed our policy"; "you arrived at a conclusion without first describing the problem." These are all examples of specific positive or corrective feedback.

Notice we have used the term "corrective" rather than the term "negative" feedback. We define negative feedback as either vague negative statements ("that's not what I want") or statements that are focused on the person rather than the person's behavior. "You're a negative influence," "You're incompetent," and "I am tired of listening to you" are all examples of negative feedback. Negative feedback is punishing to the performer and *never* appropriate. Corrective feedback provides the performer with specific information on what he or she should continue to do, stop doing, or do in place of another response. Whenever possible, a strategy of "not this, but instead that" is a far better strategy than simply saying, "No, not that."[51] In rare cases, usually when a behavior poses a threat to the performer or others, it is necessary to tell someone to stop a behavior. For example, "You have been convicted of a DUI while traveling on company business. That behavior is totally unacceptable." However, in the vast majority of cases, it is appropriate to tell a person what not to do *and* to inform them of what they should do in its place. "When a member calls with a concern, do not tell him that it's not your area of responsibility and transfer the call. Take down all the pertinent information and assure him you will have an answer for him within 24 hours or less." Replacing an undesired behavior with a desired behavior is, whenever possible, a far more effective strategy than merely telling someone what behavior you do not want.

FORMATIVE EVALUATION

The purpose of formative evaluation is to improve the probability that performance at each level of the organization results in success. It is much more frequent and often much less formal than summative evaluation.[52] Those engaged in formative evaluation (supervisors, managers, committee chairs, volunteer leaders) are focused on ensuring the organization is doing the right things right and correcting problems as they arise.

We have defined a problem as a critical difference between what is and what should be. Formative evaluation is about providing feedback to achieve a match between the two. As seen in Figure 7.1, the process of formative evaluation involves searching for gaps between what is planned (the should) and what actually occurs (the is).

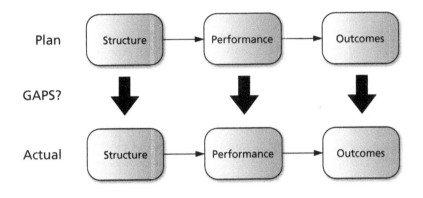

Figure 7.1 Formative evaluation model.

When a gap is identified, managers have the following options:[53]

1. *Ignore the gap.* A problem involves a critical gap, but not all gaps are problems. If the management decides to ignore a gap, it has reached the conclusion that the existence of the gap will not affect the achievement of a successful outcome. The best way to determine whether a gap is critical is to ask: What will happen if we ignore the gap? If the consequences of ignoring the gap are not harmful, leave it alone. For example, an organization might have as an objective having 80% of its members satisfied with their membership. The data reveal that 78.5% are satisfied. The board may decide that this "is" is close enough and ignore the gap.

2. *Bring "is" in compliance with "should."* When monitoring performance points to a critical gap (one that cannot be ignored), the second question to ask is: Are we capable of changing the current status to be in line with our plan (the should)? How long will it take? How much will it cost? Is the effort (and associated cost) to bring reality into alignment with the plan worth the potential benefit the organization will realize if we make the change? If the answer is "yes," then it is probably best to make the required changes. If not, consider the next option.

3. *Alter the statement of "should."* The original plan was based upon the best information available at the time the plan was developed. Feedback has provided the organization with new information indicating that the requisite structure and/or performance is not possible. What is possible with the resources that are available and the performance that can be conducted with those resources? Can the objective be modified to achieve a smaller gain than that originally intended? For example, perhaps the organization originally projected a 6% gain in member retention over a three-

year period. Six months into the plan, information now makes it clear that the organization will not have the resources and, thus, will not achieve the performance originally planned. Given the resources and resulting performance now available, can the organization project an increase in retention that is less ambitious than the original 6%? Perhaps, given the new information, a 4% or 5% target over a three-year period might be more achievable. If so, revise the target. It makes no sense to wait three years to discover the original objective cannot be achieved when the organization has data indicating it is not likely to occur.

Conversely, the organization might find it has more resources available and thus an increase in the target is warranted. The lesson here is that targets are set with the best information available. Once better information is available, it is only appropriate—in fact mandatory—to make those adjustments if the organization wishes to operate in the realm of reality. If adjustments to the target are not feasible, or if the change required is not worth the predicted benefit, then organizations are wise to consider the fourth option.

4. *Eliminate the objective.* Don Quixote is a loveable fictional character, but there is nothing admirable in either for-profit or non-profit organizations attempting to "reach the unreachable star." It is certainly appropriate to motivate performers within the organization to achieve better results than they have in the past. Such targets are appropriately called "stretch" targets. They are within our reach if we exert additional effort.

But attempting to achieve the unattainable is not motivating; in fact, it's quite the opposite. It is demoralizing. The research in performance improvement clearly teaches us that when performers view targets as unachievable, performance declines and morale suffers.[54] Wise organizations know when to cut their losses and shift their focus to other more attainable objectives. Mediocre and poorly managed organizations stubbornly hang on despite what the data reveal.

Formative evaluation involves an ongoing effort to identify gaps between what structure and performance *should be* in place and what *is* actually in place. When corrective action is warranted, it is taken. Objectives and targets are modified. When corrective action is not feasible, or when the cost/benefit ratio is not favorable, organizations don't continue to beat their heads against the wall. They don't blame or threaten performers or exhort them to try harder. Rather, they set their sights on other objectives more worthy of their effort.

Exercise 7.3

Identify a current gap concerning one of your organization's objectives. Working with your organizational leaders, analyze each of the options above (1-4) and select the one that is best for handling the identified gap.

_____

_____

_____

Formative Evaluation at the Functional Unit Level

Organizations often misunderstand the concept of *team*. All teams are groups, but not all groups are teams. A team is a group of people who, working together, produce what none of them could produce independently. Each member has a definable role that is critical to the success of the team. Team members are not always working together, but they are always working toward a common end. In effective teams, each member shares consequences of the team's actions.

Effective team performance involves individual members sharing their individual skills to produce a desired outcome. Groups composed of individuals who come together to share their ignorance only produce more of the same on a larger level. Certainly teams may be faced with problems to which they have no immediate answer. However, successful teams are composed of individuals with the skills and abilities to produce an effective answer. The old saying "two heads are better than one" is not always true. Performance literature demonstrates that when team members lack critical skills, those deficits are not removed by adding several incompetent people to work on a task. Perhaps "two heads are better than one" should be replaced with "one full head is better than 100 empty ones."

The important implication is that organizations must clearly understand what skills and abilities will be required to produce a particular outcome and assure they have selected the person or persons who have those skills. This principle becomes particularly challenging for associations and other non-profit organizations that rely on volunteers to perform critical tasks. In these cases, it is important, for a host of reasons, to involve volunteers as much as possible. However, asking volunteers to complete tasks for which they have no skill or ability is to ensure failure both for the individuals involved and for the organization. Long gone are the days when volunteers could be selected as a "reward" for service or because they were friends or associates of those in leadership positions. Today, effective organizations select volunteers to serve on the basis of merit, past performance, and demonstrated/evaluated skills and abilities.

Exercise 7.4

It is critical to ensure that team members have the skills and abilities needed to complete assigned tasks. For this exercise, identify a task or objective to be assigned to a staff or volunteer team and complete the following table. List the team members in the left column and the skills needed to complete the objective in the each column of the top row. Starting with the first team member, place an "*x*" in each cell that corresponds to the skill(s) that team member possesses. Repeat the process for each team member. If any skill does not have an "*x*" in one of the cells, a team member must be found who has that skill. If someone has no "*x*" in any of the columns, the individual should be removed from that team.

Team Members	Skill 1	Skill 2	Skill 3	Skill 4

Formative evaluation at the functional unit level basically involves the same process as formative evaluation at the organizational level. The members of the functional unit or team continue to look for gaps between their actual structural resources and performance and what was planned. To the extent possible, they close those gaps. However, functional units do not have the same level of decision-making authority as leaders in charge of organizational outcomes. Teams cannot decide, on their own, to change a target or eliminate an objective. If certain critical structural support (e.g., appropriate budget support) is lacking, teams are not in a position to secure those resources on their own. Senior management must ensure that systems are in place to allow for clear and timely communication between and among teams and with senior management so that problems can be identified as they occur and corrective action can take place. Systems should also be in place to allow teams of volunteers to provide volunteer leaders with the same information.

Formative Feedback at the Individual Level

We have noted that the purpose of summative evaluation is to increase performance. Feedback, therefore, should be as immediate as possible. The purpose of formative evaluation is to improve performance; feedback should be given when the performer is ready to receive it *and* put it into action.[55] For example, many organizations hold a debriefing shortly after the conclusion of their annual meeting to review what went well and what needs changing. At that point people are tired and not necessarily open to feedback, particularly if it is negative. The best time to talk about implementing improvements is right before they are implemented. In the example above, it would be better if people were asked to take careful notes of their thoughts about the good, the bad, and the ugly *as soon after the meeting as possible*. The time to have the "debriefing" is just before work begins on the next annual meeting. In this way, people can receive feedback and put it into practice right away.

Corrective individual feedback should be given privately, whenever possible. Correcting a performer in front of others is punishing for the performer and demoralizing for those witnessing it. Those individuals will do all they can to escape or avoid finding themselves in similar embarrassing situations in the future. As we have discussed, escape and avoidance are not healthy behaviors in an organization.

Formative feedback works best when it is given privately *and* when the performer is open to receiving it. The feedback should be specific and inform the performer on what performance is expected (the *should*) versus what performance was observed. The performer is now able to recognize the problem (the gap between what should be done and what was done). The supervisor can then engage the performer in conversation about how to close the gap. Remember that the vast majority of performance problems are not the fault of the performer, but rather the structure. The supervisor and performer should work together to determine whether any organizational impediments prevented proper performance. Was the performer lacking resources? Training? Did the performer have sufficient time? Was the desired performance communicated clearly?

Also, as we have mentioned, in discussing performance issues it is important to inform performers of what they should stop doing and to point out what they should do (not *that*, but *this*). Equally important is allowing the performer time to practice the "right way." Feedback that cannot be used is useless. Telling someone today what they need to do three months from now is not effective. Tell them three months from now and they will have an immediate opportunity to put the feedback to use. If there won't be a "next time," don't give the feedback; it will serve no positive purpose.

SUMMARY

Organizations are open systems. Open systems use information and feedback to make necessary adjustments and corrections in order to increase the probability of a successful outcome. Feedback has two purposes: to improve the probability of success (formative) and to increase the frequency of successful performance (summative).

Summative feedback is typically more formal and should be given as close to the completion of performance as practical. Formative evaluation is more informal and should be given when performers have the ability to use it. Performers should receive formative feedback in private; its purpose is to improve, not to scold, blame, or demoralize. Feedback (both formative and summative) works best when it is specific and focused on the performance, not the performer.

As you can see from this chapter and the ones preceding it, the elements of a systems approach are simple and straightforward—OPS: outcomes, performance, structure. Managing these simple components is a complex and time-consuming task. There is no shortcut and there are no magic bullets. As Jim Collins discovered, great organizations involve disciplined people doing disciplined things in a disciplined way.

Organizations that take on too much—that become activity driven rather than outcome driven—will not achieve excellence. Excellence is the consequence of a razor-like focus on mission, a limited number (six or fewer) of organizational objectives, clearly articulated strategies that involve the coordinated effort of all functional units, and commitment to ensure that performers have the tools they need and the proper environment in which to perform. Finally, these organizations consistently use feedback to make corrections at each level of OPS—altering structure where needed, correcting performance as necessary, and, when required, facing the cold, hard facts and eliminating the pursuit of outcomes out of their reach.

Easy? Not only "no" but "hell no!" Worth it? Not only "yes" but "hell yes!"

BALDRIGE CRITERIA
SUGGESTIONS AND QUESTIONS

In an effort to improve individual and organizational feedback and learning, the Baldrige Criteria for Performance Excellence ask you to consider the following questions when developing your feedback and evaluation model:

- How does your workforce feedback and performance management system support high-performance work and workforce engagement, and reinforce your business focus (objectives) in the achievement of your action plans?

- How do you assess workforce engagement?

- What formal and informal assessment methods and measures do you use to determine workforce feedback, engagement, and satisfaction?

- How do you assess workforce feedback on an organizational, departmental, and personal level; what systems do you use; and what integration methods do you use to ensure appropriate evaluation and feedback?

- How do you use feedback at all levels to stimulate organizational innovation?

The answers to the questions in this chapter and the preceding chapters will ensure that your organization is using consistently the principles of OPS and that you are moving the organization toward a higher level of outcomes expected of a highly disciplined and professional organization.

End Notes

1. Michael E. Gallery, Sherry Katamidas, and Sandra Sabo. "Measures of Success: Testing conventional wisdom." *Journal of Association Leadership,* Volume 3, Number 4, 2006.

2. James C. Collins and Jerry I. Porras, *Built to Last* (New York: Harper Business, 1997).

3. James C. Collins, *Good to Great* (New York: Harper Business, 2001).

4. James C. Collins, *Good to Great and the Social Sectors: A Monograph to Accompany Good to Great* (New York: Harper Business, 2005).

5. The American Society of Association Executives, *7 Measures of Success: What Remarkable Associations Do That Others Don't* (Washington D.C.: The American Society of Association Executives, 2005).

6. National Institute of Standards and Technology, *2013–2014 Criteria for Performance Excellence* (Gaithersburg, MD: National Institute of Standards and Technology, 2013).

7. Karl Ludwig von Bertalanffy. *General System Theory: Foundations, Development, Applications, Revised Edition* (New York: George Braziller, Inc., 1969).

8. Roger M. Addison and Carol Haig. "The performance architect's essential guide to the performance technology landscape," *Performance Improvement,* Volume 45, Issue 10, November/December 2006, 38–47.

9. Abbas Darabi. "Systems thinking and systematic methodology a semi-empirical experience in support of the ISPI value proposition," *Performance Improvement,* Volume 42, Issue 1, January 2003, 17–23.

10. Paul Niven. *Balanced Scorecard Step-by-Step: Maximizing Performance and Maintaining Results,* 2nd Edition (Hoboken, NJ: John Wiley & Sons Inc., 2006).

11. Robert S. Kaplan and David P. Norton. *The Balanced Scorecard: Translating Strategy into Action* (Boston: Harvard Business School Press, 1996).

12. George T. Doran, "There's a S.M.A.R.T. way to write management's goals and objectives." *Management Review,* Volume 70, Issue 11(AMA FORUM), 1981, 35–36.

13. Sharon L. Gander. "Beyond mere competency: Measuring proficiency with outcome proficiency indicator scales," *Performance Improvement,* Volume 45, Issue 4, April 2006, 38–44.

14. Michael Gallery and Susan Waters. "The development of consensus guidelines for strategic planning in associations," *Journal of Association Leadership,* Summer, 2008.

15. Society for Human Resource Management. *The Essentials of Strategy* (Cambridge: Harvard Business School Press, 2006).

16. Ibid.

17. Albert Hunphrey. "SWOT Analysis for Management Consulting." *SRI Alumni Newsletter* (December 2005).

18. Society for Human Resource Management. *The Essentials of Strategy* (Cambridge: Harvard Business School Press, 2006).

19. Ibid.

20. Ibid.

21. Wallace Clark and Henry Gantt. *The Gantt chart, a working tool of management.* (New York: Ronald Press, 1922).

22. W. Fazar. "Program Evaluation and Review Technique," *The American Statistician,* Vol. 13, No. 2, (April 1959), p.10.

23. The American Society of Association Executives, *7 Measures of Success: What Remarkable Associations Do That Others Don't* (Washington D.C.: The American Society of Association Executives, 2005).

24. Peter J. Fadde and Gary A. Klein. "Deliberate performance: Accelerating expertise in natural settings," *Performance Improvement,* Volume 49, Issue 9, October 2010, 5–14.

25. Patricia L. Newbold. "Why the language of work is not our best model," *Performance Improvement,* Volume 50, Issue 9, October 2011, 20–25.

26. Joan Conway Dessinger, James L. Moseley, and Darlene M. Van Tiem. "Performance improvement/HPT model: Guiding the process." *Performance Improvement,* Volume 51, Issue 3, March 2012, Pages: 10–17.

27. Danny G. Langdon. "The language of work," in Harold Stolovitch and Erica Keeps (Eds). *Handbook of Human Performance Technology* (San Francisco: Josey-Bass/Pfeiffer, 1999).

28. Tony O'Driscoll. "Chronicling the emergence of human performance technology." *Performance Improvement,* Volume 42, Issue 6, July 2003, 9–22.

29. Danny Langdon. *The Language of Work* (Human Resource Development Press, 1995).

30. Donald P. Schwab, Herbert G. Heneman III, Thomas A. DeCotiis. "Behaviorally anchored rating scales: a review of the literature." *Personnel Psychology,* Volume 28, Issue 4, pages 549–562, December 1975.

31. Travis C. Tubre and Judith M. Collins "Jackson and Schuler (1985) Revisited: a meta-analysis of the relationships between role ambiguity, role conflict, and job performance." *Journal of Management,* February 2000; Vol. 26, 1: 155-169.

32. Patricia L. Newbold. "Why the language of work is not our best model," *Performance Improvement,* Volume 50, Issue 9, October 2011, 20–25.

33. Paul H. Elliott. "Job Aids," in Harold Stolovitch and Erica Keeps (Eds). *Handbook of Human Performance Technology.* (San Francisco: Josey-Bass/Pfeiffer, 1999).

34. Robert F. Mager and Peter Pipe. *Analyzing Performance Problems: Or, You Really Oughta Wanna—How to Figure out Why People Aren't Doing What They Should Be, and What to do About It* (Atlanta: The Center for Effective Performance, 1997).

35. Vathsala Wickramasinghe and Sampath Dabere. "Effects of performance-based financial incentives on work performance: A study of technical-level employees in the private sector in Sri Lanka." *Performance Improvement Quarterly,* Volume 25, Issue 3, pages 37–51, 2012.

36. Steven J. Condly, Richard E. Clark, and Harold D. Stolovitch. "The Effects of Incentives on Workplace Performance: A Meta-analytic Review of Research Studies." *Performance Improvement Quarterly,* Volume 16, Issue 3, September 2003, 46–63.

37. Alyce M. Dickinson "Are we motivated by money? some results from the laboratory." *Performance Improvement,* Volume 44, Issue 3, March 2005, 18–24.

38. Ibid.

39. Ibid.

40. Piers Steel and Rhiannon MacDonnell. "When rewards go wrong: A tale of five motivational misdirects." *Performance Improvement,* Volume 51, Issue 8, 2012.

41. Daniel L. Stufflebeam and Anthony J. Shinkfield. *Evaluation Theory, Models, and Applications* (Hoboken, New Jersey: John Wiley & Sons, 2011).

42. Donald Tosti and Stephanie Jackson. "Feedback" in Harold Stolovitch and Erica Keeps (Eds). *Handbook of Human Performance Technology* (San Francisco: Josey-Bass/Pfeiffer, 1999).

43. Ibid.

44. B. F. Skinner. *Science and Human Behavior* (New York: The Free Press, 1953).

45. Peter M. Senge. *The Fifth Discipline: The Art and Practice of the Learning Organization* (New York: Random House, Inc. 2006).

46. Ingrid Guerra-López and Alisa Hutchinson "Measurable and Continuous Performance Improvement: The Development of a Performance Measurement, Management, and Improvement System." *Performance Improvement Quarterly,* Volume 26, Issue 2, 2013, 159–173.

47. Lauren Crigler, Alfredo L. Fort, et al. "Training Alone Is Not Enough." *Performance Improvement Quarterly,* Volume 19, Issue 1, March 2006, 99–116.

48. Robin S. Codding, Adam B. Feinberg, Erin K. Dunn, and Gary M. Pace. "Effects Of Immediate Performance Feedback On Implementation Of Behavior Support Plans." *Journal of Applied Behavioral Analysis.* 2005 Summer; 38(2): 205–219.

49. Iris Stuart. "The impact of immediate feedback on student performance: an exploratory study in Singapore." *Global Perspectives on Accounting Education,* Volume 1, 2004, 1-15.

50. Donald Tosti and Stephanie Jackson. "Feedback" in Harold Stolovitch and Erica Keeps (Eds). *Handbook of Human Performance Technology.* (San Francisco: Josey-Bass/Pfeiffer, 1999).

51. Ibid.

52. Roger A. Kaufman and Fenwick W. English. *Needs Assessment: Concept and Application.* Englewood Cliffs, New Jersey: Educational Technology Publications, 1979).

53. Ibid.

54. Patricia L. Newbold. "Why the language of work is not our best model." *Performance Improvement,* Volume 50, Issue 9, October 2011.

55. Donald Tosti and Stephanie Jackson. "Feedback" in Harold Stolovitch and Erica Keeps (Eds). *Handbook of Human Performance Technology.* (San Francisco: Josey-Bass / Pfeiffer, 1999).

Index

Page numbers in *italics* refer to figures or tables.

V

W-Z

The Knowledge Center
www.asq.org/knowledge-center

Learn about quality. Apply it. Share it.

ASQ's online Knowledge Center is the place to:

- Stay on top of the latest in quality with Editor's Picks and Hot Topics.

- Search ASQ's collection of articles, books, tools, training, and more.

- Connect with ASQ staff for personalized help hunting down the knowledge you need, the networking opportunities that will keep your career and organization moving forward, and the publishing opportunities that are the best fit for you.

Use the Knowledge Center Search to quickly sort through hundreds of books, articles, and other software-related publications.

www.asq.org/knowledge-center

Ask a Librarian

<u>Did you know?</u>

- The ASQ Quality Information Center contains a wealth of knowledge and information available to ASQ members and non-members

- A librarian is available to answer research requests using ASQ's ever-expanding library of relevant, credible quality resources, including journals, conference proceedings, case studies and Quality Press publications

- ASQ members receive free internal information searches and reduced rates for article purchases

- You can also contact the Quality Information Center to request permission to reuse or reprint ASQ copyrighted material, including journal articles and book excerpts

- For more information or to submit a question, visit **http://asq.org/knowledge-center/ask-a-librarian-index**

Visit www.asq.org/qic for more information.

The Global Voice of Quality™

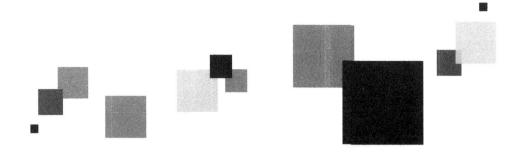

Belong to the Quality Community!

Established in 1946, ASQ is a global community of quality experts in all fields and industries. ASQ is dedicated to the promotion and advancement of quality tools, principles, and practices in the workplace and in the community.

The Society also serves as an advocate for quality. Its members have informed and advised the U.S. Congress, government agencies, state legislatures, and other groups and individuals worldwide on quality-related topics.

Vision

By making quality a global priority, an organizational imperative, and a personal ethic, ASQ becomes the community of choice for everyone who seeks quality technology, concepts, or tools to improve themselves and their world.

ASQ is...

- More than 90,000 individuals and 700 companies in more than 100 countries

- The world's largest organization dedicated to promoting quality

- A community of professionals striving to bring quality to their work and their lives

- The administrator of the Malcolm Baldrige National Quality Award

- A supporter of quality in all sectors including manufacturing, service, healthcare, government, and education

- YOU

Visit www.asq.org for more information.

ASQ Membership

Research shows that people who join associations experience increased job satisfaction, earn more, and are generally happier*. ASQ membership can help you achieve this while providing the tools you need to be successful in your industry and to distinguish yourself from your competition. So why wouldn't you want to be a part of ASQ?

Networking

Have the opportunity to meet, communicate, and collaborate with your peers within the quality community through conferences and local ASQ section meetings, ASQ forums or divisions, ASQ Communities of Quality discussion boards, and more.

Professional Development

Access a wide variety of professional development tools such as books, training, and certifications at a discounted price. Also, ASQ certifications and the ASQ Career Center help enhance your quality knowledge and take your career to the next level.

Solutions

Find answers to all your quality problems, big and small, with ASQ's Knowledge Center, mentoring program, various e-newsletters, *Quality Progress* magazine, and industry-specific products.

Access to Information

Learn classic and current quality principles and theories in ASQ's Quality Information Center (QIC), *ASQ Weekly* e-newsletter, and product offerings.

Advocacy Programs

ASQ helps create a better community, government, and world through initiatives that include social responsibility, Washington advocacy, and Community Good Works.

Visit www.asq.org/membership for more information on ASQ membership.

*2008, The William E. Smith Institute for Association Research

The Global Voice of Quality™